$4.83

The cost to impact the
life of a child for a year
...maybe forever.

Jenn Tarbell, Lance Wood
with Celina Kim

Endorsements

"The children we meet in the pages of this book remind me of the children I meet every day that I am with VisionFund's micro-entrepreneurs: they are full of unrealized potential. This book will break your heart and mend it again because when parents and carers have the confidence and the means to develop small businesses, children thrive. That does not take much: a micro-loan, a safe place for savings, some financial education, and determination. Citing a multitude of case studies, Jenn and Lance show that microfinance done well—when children's well-being is the ultimate aim—brings lasting transformation for the micro-entrepreneur and smallholder farmer and for all the children they care for. This book is essential reading for anyone interested in the spiritual aspect of economic development amongst the most vulnerable people in the world."

Michael Mithika
President & CEO of VisionFund International

"Emotional, gripping, inspiring—Jenn and Lance do an impeccable job representing and making a case for a multitude of organizations and the remarkable work they do to change the lives of children through Christ-centered micro-enterprise development."

Dave Valle
Former CEO and Founder of Esperanza International,
Baseball Broadcaster at the MLB Network

"In the stories Jenn and Lance share, you'll hear how a simple investment and encounter with Christ transforms lives and impacts children. This book will sharpen your perspective, inviting you to consider what it takes to change a child's life—and perhaps yours—forever."

Peter Greer
President and CEO of HOPE International

"A compelling case for anyone interested in helping children in the majority world—this is a must read if you're hoping to influence global change in a highly efficient way with your charitable efforts."

Chris Crane
Executive Chairman & Co-Founder of Edify

"I'll never forget the first time that I learned about HOPE International. I was driving my car listening to a podcast interview with Peter Greer, HOPE's President. Halfway through his time, he stopped and said that 'at HOPE, we don't think it's enough to alleviate financial poverty, we want to be involved in the alleviation of spiritual poverty as well.' I almost wrecked my car. I had found the organization that hit all the things for me: supporting entrepreneurs, providing dignity rather than dependency, and all in a way that loved on people and made God the hero of the story. I'm grateful for that original podcast I heard ten years ago, just like I'm grateful for this book from Jenn and Lance. Buy it, read it, share it, get involved. I promise you it'll make a difference ... maybe mostly in you."

Henry Kaestner
Managing Principal in Sovereign's Capital

Dedication

To kids around the world who suffer as a result of the social
and economic effects from global crises like COVID-19. We know
those of you living in poverty feel it the most. We will fight for you.

Contents

Foreword

Many years ago, I experienced a particularly grueling three-week international business trip. It started with a horrible case of food poisoning in China. That, combined with routine jet lag, meant I didn't sleep well for days.

By the time my plane touched down in Jakarta, Indonesia for a final round of meetings, I felt exhausted. In the taxi on the way to the hotel, I tried to study my notes for the next meeting, but I couldn't focus. The traffic had backed up and a thick haze filled the air. I missed my wife. I missed home. And I desperately wanted to sleep.

In the midst of my pity party, I felt a gentle urge to look up from my notes. A few feet away from my taxi, now at a standstill in the Jakarta gridlock, stood five barefoot boys in tattered clothes, playing in a puddle of black water. They were sailing dented cans, like ships on the ocean. And they were having *fun* doing it, giggling and laughing and splashing.

When they saw me watching them, they ran to the taxi and slapped their hands on my window. I rolled it down and we exchanged "Hi's." They weren't begging, but simply enjoying a light moment with an interested stranger. As the taxi started to slowly move on, they gave me a final wave and went back to their boat races in the dirty puddle.

By then, my mind was no longer fixated on my so-called trials. It felt as though God were saying, "Those boys seem joyful—what's *your* problem?" Whenever I'm feeling sorry for myself, I remember those kids in Jakarta. They taught me a lesson about finding joy outside of my circumstances.

Even so, no one could deny they lived in dire circumstances and in abject poverty. Whatever became of them? Did they have siblings or parents, or were the streets their only home? Where are they today? Did any of them even survive? The odds are not in their favor. Jakarta hosts one of the world's largest and most densely populated slums, a place where clean water, healthy food, shelter, and other things we take for granted hardly exist.

Our mission at Focus on the Family is to help families thrive in Christ. Whether in prosperous western nations or in the developing world, the strength and stability of the family is one of the key indicators of a society's health.

But when we turn to low- and middle-income countries in the developing world, we find another key factor to consider—and that's what $4.83 is all about. In fact, the authors of this book, Jenn and Lance, have developed an equation to help illustrate this idea:

Parent(s)+Opportunity = Kids Win.

When you live in a country with limited access to safe drinking water and sanitation, or high levels of pollution, or frequent outbreaks of disease or civil unrest, or a generally poor infrastructure, having one or both of your parents in the picture can take you only so far. Family stability is critical in these settings, of course, but a host of other issues also must be addressed. This is where the "opportunity" section of the equation comes in.

Jenn and Lance propose that one of the most effective and redemptive forms of opportunity for kids in developing nations is *Christ-centered microfinance*. Investopedia defines microfinance as "a type of banking service provided to unemployed or low-income individuals or groups who otherwise would have no other access to financial services. The goal of microfinance is to ultimately give impoverished people an opportunity to become self-sufficient."[1] If you've read about girls who have been rescued from the sex trade and empowered and trained to make purses or jewelry, or community churches in developing nations that have received small grants to start training programs for youth— *that's* microfinance.

Creating jobs and income for adults is only the tip of the iceberg, though. Christ-centered microfinance in the developing world not only builds up adults and betters communities, but it also empowers children. *Especially* children!

As you'll soon read, Christ-centered microfinance projects help to create improved housing in the Dominican Republic, provide adequate healthcare in Malawi, offer sufficient food in the Philippines, strengthen post-disaster rebuilding efforts in Haiti, and foster spiritual growth for adults and children alike in Ukraine, among many other things.

This is not about simple charity. Christ-centered microfinance empowers underserved communities—rather than giving handouts, it creates self-sustaining businesses. As the title of this book reveals, $4.83 is all it takes "to impact the life of a child for a year—maybe forever."

But don't take my word for it. Read the incredible stories in this book and discover for yourself how this innovative combination of business and ministry impacts lives and brings hope to families around the world. And maybe pray about how God might be nudging *you* to get involved in what He's doing through microfinance.

I pray that those boys I encountered in Jakarta all those years ago somehow got the opportunity to rise above their circumstances. I hope someone took the time to empower them to thrive and excel. Millions of children around the world are desperate for that!

You don't have to travel outside the U.S. to make an impact on these precious kids. By supporting organizations engaged in the mission of Christ-centered microfinance, you can make a direct investment in bettering the lives of children and families physically and spiritually. This book will show you how.

Jim Daly

President, Focus on the Family

Chapter One

Parent(s) + Opportunity = Kids Win

Which weighs more: a pound of feathers or a pound of gold?

If you said, "a pound of feathers," then maybe you haven't had your morning cup of coffee. And if you said, "a pound of gold," well, you've been bamboozled by this classic schoolyard joke.

In fact, *a pound of gold weighs exactly the same as a pound of feathers.*

But do the two have the same value? Not at all! While a pound is a pound regardless of the item being weighed, a pound of gold has far more value than a pound of feathers. Similarly, the value of a dollar can vary greatly depending on how it is spent. A dollar spent in microfinance to improve the life of a child, rather than on something ordinary, is as precious as gold. Herein lies the genius of microfinance.

But what is microfinance? And how has it proven itself to be effective?

How Does Microfinance Alleviate Poverty?

In the 1990s, the World Bank asked more than 60,000 men and women living in poverty to describe poverty in their own words. Rather than focusing on material need, the interviewees described the "shame, inferiority, powerlessness, humiliation, fear, hopelessness, depression, social isolation, and voicelessness" poverty brings.[1] Poverty extends far beyond material lack, and arguably much of it stems from lack of opportunity. Global crises often make matters worse. In 2020, for example, the COVID-19 pandemic further intensified the lack of opportunity for the impoverished.[2]

The Western world, by contrast, is ripe with opportunity. With endless opportunities to take out loans, open savings accounts, apply for credit cards, and mortgage a home, it's easy to take for granted the banking services at our fingertips. The endless mailers offering dazzlingly low rates and extra bonus points for signing up are enticing at best and annoying at worst. While it's hard to imagine those in lower income countries having no access to any kind of credit or capital, about 1.7 billion adults remain unbanked.[3] But there's hope. This is where microfinance comes in—it's banking for the unbanked.

Microfinance offers dignity and hope to men and women living in poverty by providing a safe place to save money or offering loans

to start or expand businesses. It dignifies the unbanked and materially poor who have largely been shunned by traditional banking, either intentionally or unintentionally. It invests in their ideas, dreams, and talents. It stands behind the significance, worth, and pride found in work and in being able to provide for oneself and one's family.

Two Basic Forms

Microfinance offers financial services to men and women around the world, but it often looks different from one country—or even one community—to another.

14

With *microloans,* clients receive a loan to start or expand their small business. These clients usually have no access to banking, no collateral, no credit, and would otherwise never qualify for a traditional loan. Loans as small as $100 have paved a path for millions of men and women around the world to move toward provision, dignity, independence, and freedom from extreme poverty.[4] Through microfinance, people use small amounts of seed capital to fund viable businesses such as selling tomatoes, baking bread, or sewing school uniforms.

> Microfinance dignifies the unbanked and materially poor who have largely been shunned by traditional banking, either intentionally or unintentionally. It invests in their ideas, dreams, and talents.

While the landscape of microfinance—especially through microloans—continues to change, microloans were initially rooted in community. Men and women would create a trusted loan group comprised of members from their community who agreed to "cross-guarantee" their loans. This means if, in a group of five members, one woman couldn't make that week's payment, the other four would be responsible to pay it. This rule encouraged a very careful selection of group members and created a strong incentive for mutual support after funding.

The men and women in these solidarity groups not only would support each other in their businesses, but also strengthen each other through relationship. Men and women alike share testimonies of how their solidarity group renewed their joy, their courage, and their hope.

In many organizations that employ such a microloan strategy, the loan payback ratio exceeds 97 percent.[5,6] When the interest income on the loans fully covers all costs of the program, the entire program becomes operationally self-sufficient, allowing future contributions to increase the available loan pool. The whole process empowers women and men to pull themselves out of poverty by running businesses that offer income, purpose, and dignity.

In another type of microfinance, *savings groups,* nonprofits organize groups that meet regularly to save money. Sometimes, each member may have only enough to save the equivalent of 10 cents per week. But as they pool their money together, they're creating a lump sum they can use for emergencies, school fees, livestock, and much more. In many cases, the savings of the group is used as a central pool of funds which gets loaned out to group members. The group agrees on interest rates and terms, and the members can invest the funds to start up or expand businesses.

As in the microloan strategy, each member has a strong incentive to support others in the group, both in business and in life. Savings group members are thereby equipped to pull themselves out of poverty, starting with as little as 10 cents at a time.

Jesus Makes it Better

Money often magnifies the condition of the human soul, which probably explains why the Bible has a lot to say about it. Scripture speaks of money and possessions more than 2,000 times![7] Money has a cunning way of revealing our nature and where our trust and comfort truly lie. As Matthew 6:21 states, "where your treasure is, there your heart will be also."[8]

> **Jesus and a job—it's what every person needs.**

Microfinance without Jesus is merely a transaction. The act of generating savings or getting a loan might not be helpful to someone who has an unhealthy relationship with money. As an example, if a person who is struggling with alcohol abuse uses a loan to create a successful business, isn't it possible they might use the proceeds to buy more alcohol? Having more money does not mean a person's character or behavior will improve. And furthermore, what good has really been accomplished if someone has "gained the world" but forfeited their soul?

Christ-centered microfinance focuses on life change. Jesus changes people's hearts and helps them use and relate to money in the way God intended. His message and His life have the power to transform.

According to a recent randomized controlled study, introducing Jesus led to the most positive life change.[9] In this study, 6,276 families in extreme poverty received life and business training. Some learned about Jesus and spiritual values, and some did not. The participants that received spiritual training not only reported they grew spiritually, but they also generated a 9.2% greater increase in household income than the others.

Christ-centered microfinance is about more than money and extends beyond a simple transaction. It puts participants on a path to economic empowerment, and shares the eternally life-changing message of the gospel. It recognizes both are required for radical personal and community transformation. Jesus and a job—it's what every person needs.

What About the Kids?

But what about the kids? I (Jenn) worked in development for several years, raising money for a Christ-centered microfinance organization. Because the target demographic for these programs is typically adults who take out loans or join savings groups, people often asked me, "But what about the kids?"

In Scripture, we see that God has a special place in His heart for children: "Let the little children come to me, and do not hinder them, for the kingdom of God belongs to such as these," Jesus says in Mark 10:14-15.[10]

In a world where we constantly hear about the vulnerability, exploitation, and oppression of children, many people feel passionate about supporting the next generation. And rightly so! UNICEF reports that approximately 385 million children live in extreme poverty, surviving on less than $1.90 per day.[11]

Hundreds of organizations provide exceptional support to children through food programs, housing, education, sponsorship, orphan care, and more. These groups step in when and where parents cannot.

But what if parents could *provide enough food* for their kids? What if they could *afford schooling?* What if they could *improve their housing?* What if parents received a hand up—not a handout—so they could, in turn, care for the needs of their children without requiring the help of a program?

> In a world where we constantly read about the vulnerability, exploitation and oppression of children, many people feel passionate about the next generation. Christ-centered microfinance provides a great solution for helping kids.

Microfinance has a powerful impact on kids. In our view, it's the most compelling part of the story. Microfinance empowers parents to provide for their kids in ways they couldn't before. In fact, VisionFund research shows that when a parent gets involved in Christ-centered microfinance, their child's life improves 99 percent of the time.[12] When parents are equipped with opportunity, kids win. Thus our formula:

$$Parent(s) + Opportunity = Kids\ Win.$$

We all have a role to play in helping to make sure that kids win! And we believe one way to help is with an investment of $4.83—enough to impact the life of a child for a year.

Why $4.83? HOPE International, a Christ-centered microenterprise development organization, reports that it costs $19.37 to serve one person in its microfinance or church-based savings program for one year.[13] According to the United Nations, an average of 4.01 people live in each household in the countries where HOPE operates.[14] When we divide $19.37 by 4.01, we learn it costs $4.83 to help one child for a year—an amazing impact on families and kids per giving dollar!

With $4.83, you could buy a large coffee, grab a medium-sized movie theater popcorn, or even pay for 30 minutes of big city downtown parking. But with that same $4.83, through Christ-centered microfinance, you could change the life of a child for a year—maybe forever. Four dollars and eighty-three cents!

While a pound of feathers may weigh the same as a pound of gold, their relative values differ enormously. Similarly, while $4.83 is $4.83 no matter how it gets spent, $4.83 spent in microfinance has much more value than $4.83 spent on something ordinary.

We invite you to explore with us ten ways that kids win through Christ-centered microfinance:

Valuing Work

Adequate Healthcare

Thriving Families

Sufficient Food

Sufficient Clothing

Basic Education

Spiritual Growth

Freedom from Trafficking

Improved Housing

Post-disaster Rebuilding

In the pages that follow, you'll hear real-life stories of parents who had the opportunity to receive a small loan or participate in savings groups through Christ-centered microfinance—and learn how it directly helped their children and families to flourish.

Chapter Two

Kids Win Through Valuing Work
Rich Foreigners

As we walked along the ocean shore in San Pedro, Dominican Republic, before sitting down for our first dinner together, the locals quickly identified us as foreigners. And not just that: by their standards, we were *rich foreigners*. The contrast between us was hard to miss. We had clean clothes and shoes; they did not. We wore handbags and carried cameras; they had plastic grocery bags or nothing at all. Before long, scores of people began asking us for money.

Because we had come to observe and encourage Christ-centered microfinance and see the importance of offering a "hand up" as opposed to a "handout," I (Jenn) advised the trip-goers to refrain from giving out money or gifts, of any sort, to anyone who might ask. It was the organization's policy, I explained. I watched as the eyes and faces of my friends and colleagues softened with compassion, mixed with feelings of guilt, sympathy, and obligation. Questions bubbled out: "Are you sure?" "How about just a little?" "But it's really nothing to me—*please?*" I held my ground and we continued our walk.

One young boy named Samuel decided to walk with us for most of the evening. This local boy, eleven years old, wore tattered clothing, a dingy backpack, and battered shoes. Despite his thin frame and hungry eyes, he asked for nothing. He seemed drawn to our group, somehow. Maybe taking a walk with us felt pleasingly out of the ordinary for him. Or maybe he hoped we would offer him something if he stuck around long enough. But when someone in the group offered him a half empty bottle of Gatorade, he responded with a look both exasperated and inquisitive: "I don't know you, you are a stranger." The look seemed to ask, *why on earth would I drink from a bottle with your germs?*

> **Bleeding hearts that lead to handouts won't help to change the mindset of entitlement . . .**

Samuel had a sweet presence about him. He seemed curious and unassuming, and he appeared to sincerely enjoy our company. Everyone wanted to figure out a proper way to help him, so before long a conversation broke out amongst us. "What if we buy him a pair of shoes?" someone asked. "His mom might take them and resell them to make a profit," I replied. Another suggested, "What if we give him some money?" I hesitated and answered, "That's the very message we *don't* want to send."

Just then, another local boy maybe thirteen years old, appeared out of nowhere. Having seen the bottle of Gatorade within reach in my friend's hand, he perceived it as an opportunity and snatched it. As he jogged away, his sneering smile suggested he had just won an epic battle. It happened so fast that I couldn't stop him, and my friend felt no need to fend him off.

I felt frustrated and explained that this was the very mentality we wanted to work against. Bleeding hearts that lead to handouts won't help to change the mindset of entitlement of this young man, a mindset likely passed on to him from parents, peers, and relatives. He had come to expect things for free and apparently believed it was okay to steal from someone who had something he wanted.

The Path to Dependency

As Bob Lupton discusses in his book, *Toxic Charity*, incidents like this often happen within a cycle of dependency.[1] First is *appreciation:* the recipient of your gift feels grateful for your generosity. Then follows *anticipation:* the recipient begins to think you'll probably be generous again. Soon enough appears *expectation:* the recipient begins to expect your gift-giving. Next comes *entitlement:* the recipient believes you owe him this gift. And finally, you create *dependency:* the recipient becomes entirely dependent on your gift-giving.

When recipients start relying on gifts, they no longer view work as necessary. They then lose the

Dominican Republic

The Dominican Republic has seen strong economic growth in recent years, with an average GDP growth rate of 5.3 percent between 1993 and 2018, and GDP per capita of $7,650.10 (2018).[2] A large gap remains in the distribution of wealth, however. The residents living in the most extreme poverty are mostly of Haitian origin.[3] The Dominican Republic has a Human Development Index ranking of 94 out of 189 countries.[4]

motivation to work and therefore miss out on the dignity and satisfaction that comes from work. Why work when you can rely on someone else to provide for your needs? That's the biggest downside to dependency.

This young boy felt entitled to that Gatorade. I don't know what events led up to him believing it was okay to steal, but somewhere along the way, he picked up false ideologies that allowed him to justify his illegitimate actions.

A Backpack Full of Surprises

That night, our conversation drifted back to Samuel, who had remained with us through the entire exchange. The contrast between the two peers struck us all, providing the perfect juxtaposition between the purpose of our trip and what would come next.

Samuel didn't speak English, but a fluent Spanish speaker in our group asked, "Samuel, what's in your backpack?" Samuel sheepishly opened the bag and revealed its contents: soap, a toothbrush, and shoe polish. He shined shoes to make money.

"Why don't we pay Samuel to clean someone's shoes?" someone in the group suggested. And I thought, *Yes! The perfect suggestion for this unique situation!*

In an ideal world, of course, Samuel would not have walked the streets at age eleven, with little to eat and only ragged clothes to wear. He would be a part of a family with the resources to pay for his schooling and provide for his needs. In poverty-stricken areas, unfortunately, this is not the reality for many children. In our situation, therefore, we did what we thought best for Samuel. We decided to pay him for a service that he felt honored to provide.

I had on a pair of closed-toe shoes, as opposed to the flip flops everyone else wore, so I was the lucky candidate. I sat down on the rail beside Samuel, removing my shoes and setting them beside him. He proudly opened his bag and meticulously began cleaning. I fought back tears as I watched Samuel carefully clean my dirty shoes and observed how attentively and thoroughly he cleaned every inch. He scrubbed and brushed and wiped and polished, leaving my $10 pair of shoes from Target looking as good as new. He blushed as we complimented his work.

All of it felt both wrong and right at the same time. I hated that he wandered the streets, could not attend school, and struggled to eat. I hated that he had to constantly think about ways to provide for himself. And yet, I loved that he had the courage, talent, and resourcefulness to make money. Samuel felt proud to earn the money we paid him. He felt dignified in knowing he had what it took to make money. He was very good at something that blessed other people. He shined shoes like an artist.

> (Samuel) felt dignified in knowing he had what it took to make money. He was very good at something that blessed other people. He shined shoes like an artist.

We paid Samuel what he had earned, said our goodbyes, and departed for dinner. Few of us spoke on our walk back, but all of us reflected on the evening and on the two young boys who had crossed our path.

The Gift of Work

I can't help but think Samuel must have observed and adopted a good work ethic from someone he respected. Perhaps his dad had a job in the sugar cane fields and his mom operated a small store, and he had watched them both work hard to make ends meet for their family. Or maybe an aunt or an uncle had a shoe shining business and gave him some leftover polish and a brush after seeing his curiosity and interest. Whatever the situation, someone in Samuel's story helped him understand the value of work. He had observed someone work hard and earn money, and he saw the dignity and opportunity that came as a result.

Or could shoe shining have been just a side gig? Maybe, as we would hope for most kids, his "work" was doing well in school, and he shined shoes only when he had time. Maybe he had excellent parents who instilled strong morals and values into him, helping him to understand that, in this world, you have to provide value in order to receive money in exchange. Perhaps his mom and dad encouraged him to find something on the side to help him save money for the toy he wanted in the store, or the bike he'd been eyeing. When I was eleven, I babysat to save some money for things I wanted. Maybe Samuel shined shoes as a means to the same end?

Whatever the case, I find it remarkable that Samuel knew better than to feel entitled. Instead, he chose to feel empowered to work hard to earn money. And in his world, after spending five minutes shining a pair of shoes, Samuel had enough money to buy his own Gatorade, as opposed to the half bottle his peer had stolen.

The opportunity to work is a gift. It's something to be grateful for. It keeps us out of a position of entitlement and dependency because it keeps our eyes focused on the opportunity to create and provide value, to think competitively, to explore innovation. With opportunity and an abundance mindset, fear and scarcity shrivel, paving the way for new ideas. And when kids learn the power of having opportunity and limitless thinking, no one can stop them.

Kids who have the privilege of observing their parents build a business receive a new lens to look through. They get to see firsthand a mom or a dad hold their head high with the pride of ownership, with the dignity that comes through creating, with the joy that results from feeling empowered. Work is a gift. The opportunity to create is God-given. We are co-creators and co-laborers with the Lord, and the opportunity to use our skills, gifts, and talents to add and create value for others as a means of providing for ourselves is part of how the Kingdom of God operates. When kids watch their parents value both work and opportunity, they learn to value them as well.

Kids Win through
Valuing Work

The United Nations (UN) states that a lack of decent work opportunities, sufficient investments, and consumption lead to an erosion of the basic social contract underlying democratic societies: that all must share in progress.[5] While the global unemployment rate has recovered from the global financial crisis of 2009, large disparities still exist across regions and age groups. In addition, having a job does not guarantee a decent living.[6] In 2018, 700 million employed workers and their families still lived in extreme or moderate poverty with less than $3.20 a day.[7] This is why the U.N. Sustainability Goal 8 focuses not just on creating jobs, but ensuring that all individuals—regardless of gender, income level, or socio-economic background—are given opportunities to have access to decent work.[8] While welfare programs allow governments to temporarily assist families in need, studies have shown that the welfare process can have a long-lasting negative effect on both current and future generations. A study in Norway found that if parents become welfare dependents, the likelihood of their children eventually becoming welfare recipients also increases.[9] Encouraging entrepreneurship and reinforcing the value of work, especially in younger generations, are key to driving progress toward sustaining economic growth, reducing forced labor, and improving living standards.

Kids win with Valuing Work through Christ-centered microfinance.

Chapter Three

Kids Win with Thriving Families
Can You Prevent a Broken Heart?

Martha Eye grew up on a small farm in southern Ethiopia with her parents, five sisters, and one brother. Their livelihood depended entirely on raising livestock and growing *enset* (similar to a banana tree), bamboo, green cabbage, and barley. She remembers the moment clearly when a serious illness struck her mother.

Her father went everywhere to find help. First, the pair visited religious healers who killed animals twice a year to shed their blood as a sacrifice to the ancestral spirits. But these men could not heal Martha's mother. Then they went to the health center near their little village of Beto Kebele. The kind people there tried intently, but they could not help her. Martha's mother continued to shiver with sickness.

Finally, out of sheer desperation, they went to a small Christian church in their village. The pastor prayed for Martha's mother, and by the power of Jesus Christ, the Lord cast out the illness that tortured her. She was healed!

In that moment, everything changed for Martha. She saw that God and Jesus are real, and that the Lord is both willing and able to heal. Not long afterward, Martha's parents and many in her family, including Martha herself, accepted Jesus Christ as their Lord and Savior.

A Teen Bride

When Martha was a teenager, her father told her she would soon marry a young man named Tune (pronounced Too-nay). Her father, with the church pastor and the village elders, had arranged it all. Martha and Tune knew very little about each other; in fact, they met for the first time on their wedding day. Standing next to Tune at the wedding ceremony, Martha's hands trembled. Still, Tune was tall and handsome, and she felt happy to marry him. She was excited about their new life together.

Once married, Martha and Tune received a small plot of land and a young cow from Tune's father as a wedding gift. Together, they farmed the land and built a small hut from sticks. It stood about eleven feet in diameter, with a small door just four feet high. They had no windows and no light inside, only a small campfire, a pot, and a few cooking utensils.

At night, their cow joined them in the hut to keep her safe from the hyenas. With no furniture in their hut, Martha and her husband slept on a bed of *enset* leaves on one side, while the cow slept on the other. It was humble, but Martha felt happy to call it home.

Martha and Tune fell into a routine, working throughout the week and walking fifteen minutes to church on Sundays, where they both volunteered and sang in the choir. Over the next several years, they had three children: a daughter, Mashure; a son, Tariku; and another son, Abreham.

To support their growing family, Tune would go to Girja, a district in the Oromia Region of Ethiopia, to work during the coffee harvest season (November through February). The family earned enough money to buy food and school supplies, send Mashure to school for part of the day, and begin plans to build a new hut. Martha had her hands full with three young children and felt excited about the future.

Rainy Season

Then, one day, as the rainy season began, life itself rained on Martha.

Ethiopia

With a population of about 109 million people, Ethiopia is the second most populous nation in Africa (2018).[1] Despite having the fastest growing economy in the region, it is among the poorest countries in Africa, with a GDP per capita of $767.56 (2017).[2] Around 26 million Ethiopians live below the poverty line on less than $1.90 a day.[3] Ethiopia is one of the least developed countries in the world, with a Human Development Index ranking of 173 out of 189 countries (2017).[4] (The Human Development Index is a measurement created by the UN to assess the development of a country beyond economic growth alone through measurements of a long and healthy life, being knowledgeable, and having a decent standard of living.)

Tune felt sick and visited the village health center. The nurse told him he had a stomach problem, maybe an ulcer, as well as a cold, so she gave him some medicine. Tune began taking the medicine and immediately returned to his routine of harvesting crops.

The following night, Tune spoke of further abdominal pain. Martha made a fire to warm him, but Tune grew progressively worse. "I feel like I am going to die," he told her. But he wouldn't allow Martha to get help. "I'm afraid that if you go outside in the middle of the night, the hyenas might attack you," he told her. "I don't want our children to lose both parents." Finally, at 4:00 a.m., Martha rushed to get Tune's family, the church pastor, and elders. They brought more medicine and began praying for Tune.

Since the villagers did not have a vehicle to take Tune to the health center in Yaye, a larger town five miles away, the men made a stretcher and carried him the whole way on foot—a grueling journey. The nurse examined Tune and immediately referred him to the hospital in Hawassa for more comprehensive treatment. The group then arranged to rent an Isuzu truck to make the 45-mile drive and sent Martha home to care for and comfort the children. Pastor Bunkara and Kumalo, Tune's brother, would transport Tune to the hospital.

On the way to Hawassa, Tune died.

The shock and grief over her husband's death overwhelmed Martha. In a matter of just a few days, her life had turned upside down. She lost all hope. "After [Tune] passed away," she said, "there was a totally black and dark time in my life. My tears and my cry were my common language to express my sorrow."

Moving On

Martha felt isolated, frightened, and without support. Although her mother came to visit, she could do little but cry because she had no resources herself to offer her daughter. Martha also suffered from another potent fear. Her old hut had a gaping hole that exposed her family to the elements and to wild animals. "I decided to sleep on the hole's side," she said, "so that even if the hyenas attacked, I would sacrifice myself for my children. Every night, I feared and worried that the hyenas might attack. I felt insecure in every aspect."

Martha had to sell one of their two cows to cover Tune's funeral expenses and other costs. With no savings, she struggled to support herself and her children. Without Tune to tend the land, the farm produced no crops. And because the farm had no fences, cows from the village trampled the land. "My farm looked like a desert," Martha recalled. "My house was too old, and cows destroyed my *enset*. I wanted to disappear from this village and go to places very far away, where I didn't have to hear about the situation I was passing through." Despite her discouragement, Martha set out to look for work.

Each day, Martha asked Mashure to take care of the cow and left Tarikut with neighbors. Then Martha carried Abreham on her back as she searched for work. She ground *enset,* prepared *kocho,* cleaned huts, and cleared away animal dung. Sometimes, the people she worked for gave her some food to take home. Despite her hunger, she did not eat it but set it aside for her children to eat in the evening. With no steady work, she had to search for scraps of food normally given to animals. When there was no other alternative, she begged for food. The weather grew bitterly cold, and Martha and her children slept on the hut's dirt floor with only *enset* leaves to keep them warm.

The Big Decision

As the days dragged on, Martha feared that if she didn't do something different, her children would die. She worried the most about Abreham. He was so small! The health workers and government administrator spoke to her about adoption. But she loved Abreham so very much. How could she give him up? The church had many widows at that time, but none of them had put their children up for adoption. *They must have others who help them,* Martha thought.

Many villagers said to her, "You should keep your son with you. If it is the will of God, he will survive, or at least he will die here." Martha prayed again and again for guidance. In her heart, Martha believed that if she did not relinquish Abreham, her beloved son would die. Finally, she met with her younger brother, and the two talked for hours. He said she alone must decide and do what she thought best. At last, she decided to give Abreham up for adoption in order to save his life.

> If I do not place him for adoption, she thought, he will definitely die. I can't let him die.

Shortly thereafter, Martha gathered her courage and took Abreham to the government office in Yaye. Her brother accompanied her. As she spoke with Chuchu, the social worker, Martha could not control her emotions. She began to weep at the thought of losing her son. Chuchu encouraged her to consider taking her son back home. But with tears streaming from her eyes, and knowing what was ultimately best for her son, Martha repeatedly insisted, "*This* is what I want." Chuchu relented, they signed the documents, and Martha agreed to return with Abreham the next day to relinquish her son.

The next day, Wednesday, July 22, 2009, Martha's family woke up early to walk to the government office together. Although Martha continued to feel conflicted, she saw no better option. *If I do not place him for adoption, she thought, he will definitely die. I can't let him die.* Mashure, ten years old at the time, remembers that day well. She loved Abreham very much. Although she often cared for him like a parent, she also counted him as her best friend. A crying Abreham would often ask her to carry him on her back to go outside. She loved to play soccer with him, using a ball they had made from dried *enset* leaves tied together. When the sheep they owned gave birth to two little lambs, they each adopted one to love and to play with.

On the way to the office, Abreham, who had just turned two years old, didn't seem to understand the significance of what was happening. He was laughing and feeling light-hearted while everyone else wiped away tears. Mashure held her brother tightly. "Do not worry," Abreham said, "I am going to the government." Again and again he said, "Mashure, please feed my sheep. Keep him safe and look after him."

As the family released Abreham, Mashure prayed for his health, for peace, and for this terrible situation to somehow have a good outcome. Martha cried the whole way back to their hut and felt sick for a week afterward. For the second time in her life, she suffered a broken heart. She prayed that a wonderful Christian family would adopt Abreham.

Prayers from the Other Side of the Globe

As Martha prayed, on the other side of the world, my (Lance's) family also prayed. My wife, Jeanie, and I had three biological children and had adopted a daughter from Ethiopia one year earlier. Now, we felt God's call to adopt another child.

We still remember the morning we made the decision to move forward. We were at Forest Home Family Camp, and we called the adoption agency from a pay phone in the stairway of the lodge. It was Wednesday, July 22, 2009—the same day Martha gave Abreham up for adoption.

We quickly completed the required clearances, social work studies, criminal background checks, and other paperwork. We had done this before and knew what to expect. In record time, we sent in our final documents. We expressed an openness to adopt a child with special needs or disabilities.

With the paperwork done, we received access to the adoption agency's special needs list. As Jeanie opened the list and viewed the many children in need of homes, she felt particularly drawn to a photo of a little boy named Abreham Tune. He was very thin and had beautiful eyes. The website said that Abreham had a heart disorder and had been diagnosed with marasmus (severe undernourishment resulting in significantly low weight for his age). As a child on the special needs list, he was eligible for fast-track adoption.

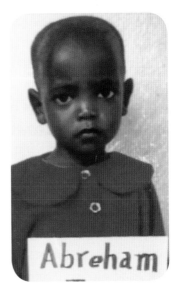

When we called the agency to express interest in Abreham, we learned his father had passed away, but it surprised us to hear that his mother was still alive. She had apparently given him up, in part, due to financial difficulties. We asked the agency if we could sponsor Abreham's family financially, pay for him to receive medical attention, and return him to his mother. We would then adopt an orphan who had no other options. Wouldn't that be a win for everyone?

After several conversations, however, we learned that the law prohibited making payments to a birth mother. Once a child was put up for adoption, that child could not return to his or her family. Not only could payments be misconstrued as "buying" children, but returning a child to his or her family might encourage other mothers to give their children up for adoption in hopes of getting their children back with added benefits. After serious pushing, we finally accepted the fact that Abreham could not return home to be with Martha.

Adoption at Light Speed

Because of Abreham's special needs, his adoption took place very quickly. Our whole family traveled to Ethiopia for "Gotcha Day" (when we first met him), which occurred in the orphanage on March 28, 2010. The adoption became final at the U.S. Embassy in Addis Ababa shortly thereafter. We changed his name to Abraham Tune Wood to reflect the more common American spelling and to honor his birth father.

On April 5, Abraham traveled with us to his new home in California. By then, because he had been fed in the orphanage, he was no longer starving, and his heart problems had subsided.

Both Martha and our family see God's fingerprints all over the adoption process. These fingerprints include Martha relinquishing on July 22, the same day we decided to adopt, and a fast track process due to special needs (which later got resolved). Not long after Abraham's adoption, international adoptions from Ethiopia closed. Had the process taken longer, he might still be in the orphanage today. The Bible says that "God causes all things to work together for good to those who love

God, to those who are called according to His purpose" (Romans 8:28). Sometimes, that "working together" involves adoption.

We are so grateful for our son, Abraham. He's a smart, funny twelve-year-old who loves sports, drums, and animals. He's been a part of our family for nearly ten years, and we can't imagine life without him.

Is it Possible to Prevent a Heart from Breaking?

Although Abraham's adoption worked out well, the process clearly caused a lot of pain and challenges for Martha and her family. Imagine the anguish of having to give up your beloved child for adoption so that he wouldn't starve to death!

What if the story had looked different? What if Martha had been part of a women's savings group and had savings set aside? What if, even after Tune died, she had received a small loan to repair her fences, close the gaping hole in her hut, and continue to grow crops to sell or to keep to provide food for her children? What if she had been supported by the prayers and encouragement of women like her? What if her local church had been equipped with the resources to more fully care for her (and others in similar situations)?

We believe stories like Martha's can look different. Of the approximately eight million children in orphanages, it is estimated that 90% have at least one living parent.[5] As skilled and hard-working parents like Martha are given opportunities and access to Christ-centered microfinance, their families can remain intact. And maybe fewer mothers in circumstances like Martha will suffer from broken hearts.

Kids Win with
Thriving Families

Nearly 385 million children live in extreme poverty, surviving on less than $1.90 per day.[6] It is estimated that there are nearly 140 million orphans globally.[7] Of the approximately eight million in orphanages, it is estimated that 90% have at least one living parent.[8] While reasons vary, it is most commonly poverty that drives families to relinquish their children to orphanages.[9] UNICEF child protection officials believe that if families could get the services they need, it could prevent children from needing alternative care from the start.[10] Through Christ-centered microfinance, parents get the opportunity to provide for their families, thereby allowing families to stay together and children to thrive.[11]

Kids win with Thriving Families through Christ-centered microfinance.

Chapter Four

Kids Win with Sufficient Clothing
Using Scars to Heal

Authorities believe about 800,000 people died in the 100-day Rwandan genocide.[1] Though the genocide happened twenty-five years ago, the memories remain a significant part of many survivors' stories—survivors like Umutesi Saudi.

Today, you might find Umutesi in a Rwandan marketplace, handing out baskets of eggs while tucking customers' payments into a fold of her gown. She expects her chicken-and-egg business to grow from 600 chickens to 4,000. A successful businesswoman, Umutesi has a college education, a home with electricity and running water, and a car. Her story is a miraculous one, despite the early scars left by the genocide.

A Four-Year-Old's Nightmare

In early April 1994, someone shot down an airplane carrying Rwandan president Juvenal Habyarimana and Burundian president Cyprien Ntaryamira, killing everyone on board and sparking the 100-day Rwandan genocide. With ethnic tensions already on the rise, Hutu extremists began slaughtering members of the Tutsi minority, as well as other Hutus considered Tutsi sympathizers. Umutesi was just four years old.

The pursuing Hutus forced Umutesi and her six siblings to run and keep on running. They crouched in swamps during the day and hid in the fields at night. Umutesi and her siblings had not seen their parents since they fled their home.

One night, as Umutesi crawled through a potato field, she raked the dirt with her hand. Grime caked under her fingernails until . . . *swfp*. Something soft brushed against her fingertips: a sweet potato, smaller than a child's palm. She dug it up and held it up to the Rwandan starlight. It was shrunken, desiccated, and bearing bruises of rottenness, yet she nearly chirped with excitement. She raised her head from the field, signaling her brothers and sisters so they could each get a nibble.

The days grumbled past like gray clouds, and the siblings continued to hunt for food together and share their treasures of rotten, bruised vegetables, whatever they could salvage from fields and trash. They passed bodies piled up beside houses, across fields, and in lakes.

Six weeks into their nightmare, Umutesi fell severely ill. Cholera? She did not know. At night, she shivered violently, struggling to keep quiet. The Hutus might hear her, find her, and slaughter her and her siblings. But to refrain from crying was not to breathe. She bit her tongue hard to keep silent, but her moans broke free and escaped into the night.

Loud voices broke out nearby—brief, staccato syllables, drowning out the chirps of the insects around her. Footsteps, heavy and booted, crunched on the dirt.

A troop of soldiers from the Rwandan Patriot Force (RPF) stumbled across the starving family, carrying knives on their belts and pointing guns. But these soldiers were not Hutu. They spoke peacefully and gently to Umutesi and her siblings and quickly led them to their camp, where a doctor tended to Umutesi's sickness. The soldiers offered the children food, and over the coming weeks, provided good care to Umutesi and her siblings.

Weeks later, Umutesi regained her strength, and the soldiers returned her and her siblings to their home.

But they did not return to a place they recognized.

After the Genocide

Her father's appearance had changed. His kind face bore ragged machete scars, and broken bones had slowed his formerly brisk gait.

Umutesi would never again see her gracious mother, who had been murdered during the bloody rampage. As time went on, Umutesi began to help with the household, cooking meals and cleaning the home. She became like a mother to her father, feeding him and bathing him. With little time to sleep, her eyelids drooped as though they had turned to lead. Her daily routine became an hourly struggle.

A year later, a glimmer of hope broke through when her father remarried. Umutesi's burden quickly grew lighter, now that her father had found someone to care for him. But before long, her father's groaning became more guttural, his wheezing wetter and deeper. Shortly after getting remarried, her father took his final breath, a belated victim of the genocide.

Rwanda

Rwanda has one of the fastest growing economies in Central Africa, with GDP growth of about 7 percent per year between 2010 and 2018, and a GDP per capita of $788 (2018).[2] Rwanda's economy has come a long way since the Rwandan genocide of 1994, in which 800,000 people were killed.[3] Although poverty has fallen significantly since the genocide, it is estimated that 53.1 percent of the population still lives under the international poverty line (2017).[4] With more than half of the population living on less than $1.90 a day, access to necessities such as clothing and shoes still proves a challenge for many families. Rwanda has a Human Development Index ranking of only 158 out of 189 countries.[5]

> While living with her aunt, Umutesi remembers wearing just one dress day and night for nearly three years until its hem unraveled and the dress looked more like tattered ribbons.

Umutesi and her six siblings moved in with an aunt. While living with her, Umutesi remembers wearing just one dress day and night for nearly three years until its hem unraveled and the dress looked more like tattered ribbons. "Things children have rights to, we did not have while growing up," Umutesi recalled. Within a few years, her aunt remarried and the siblings were forced to return to their stepmother.

Their stepmother beat them, called them insulting names, and regularly abused them. She considered new clothing an unnecessary luxury, and the three years Umutesi already had worn the dress lengthened into five. It no longer covered her properly, revealing more and more of her body.

Her three oldest siblings left: One joined the army while the other two chose to survive on the streets. Too young to follow them, Umutesi became the eldest sibling remaining at her stepmother's home. She had to fetch water from the distant hills, gather firewood, attend to the farm animals, clean the house, and prepare the family's meals.

Free to Learn

Between her daily chores and her regular beatings, Umutesi managed to finish primary school and, thanks to her good grades, ultimately had the opportunity to attend high school at a boarding institution in the Northern Province, Musanze.

Around this time, she met an attractive young man named Sentwali. And by her eleventh year of school, she became pregnant. Umutesi dropped out of school and married Sentwali. They snuggled into a small home with one bedroom and a living room. Before she gave birth, the pair moved to a home with two bedrooms, making it much more convenient to feed and take care of the baby.

Shortly thereafter, Sentwali went to work for his uncle, who in time revealed himself as an unpredictable, abusive, and domineering man. Despite the difficult work, Sentwali learned to drive and soon obtained a trucking license and a new career.

This new job promised a way out of lifelong hardship—an escape he'd never dreamed possible.

The young couple bought about half an acre of land for 600,000 Rwandan francs (rwfs; $672), on which they envisioned building their own home.

But a stampede of trials quickly altered their dreams.

From Bad Luck to Divine Blessing

Umutesi and Sentwali moved into their house before it was finished. Almost immediately, Sentwali lost both his job and his truck when the owner of the business decided to sell the business and the vehicle. At the same time, a severe case of asthma struck Umutesi, making her unable to cook, clean, or help with chores. Life grew deeply uncertain with an unfinished house, little income, ailing health, and a newborn.

Umutesi's sickness left her hospitalized. Not only did her husband have to take care of the baby, but he also had to look after his wife. "We honestly had nothing, nowhere to get food," Umutesi remembers. "But God made a way." Neighbors provided for them in their time of need.

Soon after Umutesi left the hospital, a neighbor told her about Urwego Bank, a local microfinance institution, which provided loans to women and men through trust groups. The neighbor even suggested that a very small amount of money could help transform Umutesi's family. Umutesi felt ready to jump at the opportunity, but Sentwali remained skeptical. How would they repay the loan? Where would the money come from? They might lose their unfinished house. Was the opportunity worth the risk?

Umutesi insisted on taking chances rather than sitting around and waiting for a miracle. Armed with little but determination, Umutesi attended financial literacy training offered by the bank. She also worked to gather thirty-two members to join her trust group.

For three months, the members of her group received training in financial literacy. Afterward, Umutesi received her first loan of 100,000 rwfs ($112), which she used to start an egg business.

With the loan, Umutesi bought twenty chicks and their feed, and she and Sentwali became the chicks' full-time caretakers. She befriended a neighboring chicken farmer and learned more about the business and how to care for her animals. Every once in a while, her husband received a day or two of freelance work as a driver for tourists, earning $30 per day. The couple used his earnings to pay off their loan at 7,000 rwfs ($8) per week. With discipline and perseverance, they repaid their first loan within four months.

Best of all, perhaps, their twenty chickens started laying eggs. *Lots* of eggs.

Their second loan doubled to 200,000 rwfs ($224), which they used to buy one hundred more chickens, chicken feed, medicines, and more. They quickly repaid this loan as well.

Umutesi started selling eggs both at the market and through wholesale. She also began supplying 5,000 eggs per week to five hotels, making a weekly profit of 100,000 rwfs ($106). Those sales earned her enough money to rent a business space, and in 2016, she purchased her own business property.

Today, Umutesi sells eggs and chickens to both hotels and restaurants. Through saving money and running a profitable business, Umutesi and Sentwali bought a car. They use the car to transport eggs from remote village farmers. They also installed both plumbing and electricity in their home, making their house the only one in the village with water and power.

Since that time, they've made enough income for Sentwali to build new doors for their house. Umutesi gave birth to two more children, and the couple adopted three others. Together, she and Sentwali pay for their children to attend private schools.

> How very different the lives of Umutesi's children look from her own childhood! With enough money to feed, clothe, and educate her children, Umutesi is able to provide for her family. Her kids don't worry about hungry bellies, ragged clothes, or unaffordable schooling.

How very different the lives of Umutesi's children look from her own childhood! With enough money to feed, clothe, and educate her children, Umutesi is able to provide for her family. Her kids don't worry about hungry bellies, ragged clothes, or unaffordable schooling.

No one will ever have to ask this successful businesswoman whether microfinance works.

Big Dreams, Bright Future

Today, Umutesi serves as an usher at her church and meets the needs of her community by mentoring young people. Through faith in Jesus, she uncovered the joy of forgiveness, which has, in part, enabled her and her entire family to thrive.

Working to help her family and others has become the focus of Umutesi's life and given direction to her business. Umutesi does not want any child to see her or his youth ripped away, as hers was stolen from her. So, she works. She gives. Her business flourishes, and she praises God.

In a land where hundreds of thousands of precious lives were lost in the Rwandan genocide, Umutesi Saudi has learned to live with her scars. And she is determined to use those scars to help improve the lives of her family and her community while advancing the Kingdom of God.

From literal rags to true Kingdom riches, Umutesi's story shows the multiplicative effect of capital in growing a business. Her kids felt the biggest impact. Never will they have to experience the embarrassment or shame their mom faced in wearing the same revealing dress for five years, or fighting to stay alive and unsure of who to trust. The stark contrast between her childhood and the childhood she's providing for her own children (both biological and adopted) is beyond comparison—and it all started because of a small, $112 loan.

As Umutesi and her family realized their God-given potential—in large part because someone believed in them enough to give them an opportunity through microfinance—everything changed. The days continue to dawn bright.

Kids Win with

Sufficient Clothing

Without sufficient clothing and shoes, millions are at risk for life-threatening illnesses and infections from worms and parasites. Today, more than 1.5 billion people are infected with parasitic diseases through contaminated soil.[6] Many of these infections could have been prevented by wearing proper footwear.

Unfortunately, parasitic diseases and infections have long-term consequences, sometimes resulting in amputation, damaged organs, hindered physical and mental development, and even death. Clothing and shoes act as protective barriers that reduce susceptibility to disease.

Kids win with Sufficient Clothing through Christ-centered microfinance.

This story showed how kids win through
Christ-centered microfinance in these additional areas:

Valuing Work	Improved Housing
Thriving Families	Sufficient Food
Spiritual Growth	Basic Education

Chapter Five

Kids Win with Spiritual Growth
A Beggar finds Jesus

Hardship in Ukraine

In some places within Ukraine, particularly rural areas, many children lack access to adequate food or education. Some also come from difficult home environments, leading to psychological or emotional trauma. Alcoholism runs rampant, abuse is common, and more than one in ten parents leave their children for days or weeks at a time in order to pursue work opportunities abroad.[1,2]

According to UNICEF, of the nearly eight million children in Ukraine, 430,000 face significant risks to their psychological and physical well-being.[3] Many live with psychological wounds and need ongoing support to address the emotional trauma of growing up surrounded by a prolonged conflict.[4]

At school, things may not look much different. Some instructors are only teaching for the money. They show little interest in the education and well-being of their students.[5,6]

An even worse situation afflicts Ukrainian villages.

The Roma on the Outskirts

The Roma people group lives largely on the outskirts of mainstream society, both figuratively and literally. They have been marginalized for centuries.[7] Prejudice toward the Roma seems so commonplace throughout the nation that such prejudice is often perceived as the norm.[8] In fact, widespread discrimination and repression has manifested itself in vicious anti-Roma raids that have swept the country in recent years.[9] Horrific acts of violence have gone largely unpunished, and many authorities have chosen to take a backseat rather than pursue justice.[10]

Some Ukrainians view the Roma people as a nomadic group known only for lying, stealing, and cheating. Such a negative perception creates barriers to life opportunities for the Roma community.[11] Not only that, but poverty runs rampant among the Roma. Since they typically have no education or full-time jobs, many take part-time work wherever they can.[12] Some have even moved to Hungary for months at a time to take temporary construction jobs.

Thousands of Roma children have no place to go for care, and the failing education system often leaves them illiterate.[13] With few activities to occupy them, these children sometimes resort to stealing and experimentation with dangerous substances. Police tend to remain largely uninvolved, as most villages have little police presence. Typically, one police representative oversees a region of villages.

Most Roma youth eventually leave the villages to find work. Many move to Kyiv, believing, as one local stated, that "Kyiv lives and the rest of the country survives." Even if they find work in the big city, they often continue to live in a village because living in the city costs too much.

An Unlikely Transformation

Pastor Albert is a member of the Roma community. Before he met Jesus, he was a self-described "drunkard" who kept himself, his wife, and their eight children alive by begging and stealing. All ten of his family members lived in a small room, with little means of survival. After his conversion, Albert stopped drinking and smoking. His wife remained skeptical of his transformation and waited for the other shoe to drop. But after six months, God also captivated her heart, and, shortly thereafter, she was baptized.

Albert's family stopped begging and stealing and started a small business collecting metal to recycle. He soon joined a savings group with other members in his community. His family's life steadily improved as Albert and his wife worked and earned roughly $20 per day. Soon, they had gained the resources they needed to buy food and clothing, and to provide for their children.

Albert and his wife are now the proud owners of both a home and a car. Their children have seen the life transformation that comes from making the difficult choice to

Ukraine

Ukraine, the second largest country in Europe, has a GDP per capita of $2,975.[14] It has undergone a host of political, security, and economic challenges. Despite Ukraine's independence since 1991, it still strives to fully break free from Russian control. Ukraine has experienced steady economic growth since mid-2015 after a substantial decline post the Crimea annexation.[15, 16, 17] It has a Human Development Index ranking 88 of out of 189 countries (2017).[18] Ukraine's population is mostly Christian, with two-thirds of its residents identifying themselves as Orthodox.[19] However, the communist regime's atheistic propaganda and negative publicity from the Orthodox church has created increasing distrust of evangelical churches and institutions.[20]

work hard and to take a higher road. One of their sons, now twenty-one, lives and works in Hungary, making a good living in construction and providing Albert with the opportunity to occasionally join him on a job.

Today, Albert is a pastor in a 200-family Roma community in Transcarpathia, Ukraine. Pastor Albert has a big vision for his community, a vision in which children grow up knowing the Lord and where the Roma and immigrant Hungarians (who don't normally mix) become friends and attend the same church. The church he pastors started with five people and has grown to more than fifty.

Since joining a savings group, Pastor Albert has seen the power of saving money in community. Like some other savings groups throughout the world, his group follows a "5W's" framework ("5W's": **W**elcome, **W**orship, **W**ord, **W**ork, **W**rap up; this framework originated from the Center for Community Transformation in the Philippines and has been adopted by the broader HOPE International network). The group meets two times a month to contribute to their savings.

A typical meeting begins with a greeting (**W**elcome), followed by a couple of songs familiar to the group and sometimes led by someone who plays an instrument (**W**orship). Then, Pastor Albert opens the Bible and leads a discussion from Scripture (**W**ord). Once finished, financial matters are addressed and the proper records updated (**W**ork). Finally, they close with prayer (**W**rap up).

As a result of these efforts, group members have steadily improved their quality of life through developing relationships, growing in their faith, and saving money. Additionally, they have created an emergency fund with enough resources to give some money to community members who don't have husbands or fathers.

From drunk beggar to church leader, Pastor Albert is living a transformed life. The crazy thing is that stories like Pastor Albert's are not uncommon in Christ-centered microfinance. When given an opportunity, many like him have undergone radical transformation.

Another Adventure in the Ukraine

More than twenty years ago, Paul and Cindy Marty felt God's tug to leave a comfortable lifestyle in the United States and move to Zaporozhye, Ukraine, to launch HOPE International's first microfinance program. Shortly after their arrival in 1997, they found themselves immersed in Ukrainian culture, yearning to understand the people and their way of life. They also wanted to discover the state of the church throughout the country.

While working with local entrepreneurs who had heard about Jesus through HOPE, the Martys quickly realized that very few children had opportunities to learn of their Savior. Years of indoctrination under a communist regime had instilled a fear of the evangelical church in the Ukrainian culture.[21] This has contributed to the spiritual poverty throughout the nation.

Years of indoctrination under a communist regime had instilled a fear of the evangelical church in the Ukrainian culture. This has contributed to the spiritual poverty throughout the nation.

A small spark of hope ignited a raging fire deep in the hearts of Paul and Cindy, who longed to see the children of Ukraine learn about Jesus and read the Bible. To meet a profound spiritual need in the community and the nation, they began conducting weekly Bible clubs in which children could hear the gospel, acquire new life skills (such as drawing, sewing, writing, or reading), learn to follow Jesus through relationships with godly mentors, and have fun.

And so, the Tomorrow Clubs (TC) were born.

At first, the clubs tied themselves to local churches. But as the Martys began to visit remote villages, many of them miles from the nearest local church, they saw countless children playing in the streets. Either these children had no schools, they couldn't read, or their deep poverty kept them away. In response to this tremendous need, the TC model shifted to a focus on the poor and unchurched of Ukraine.

The Vital Connection to Microfinance

The collaboration between HOPE International and Tomorrow Clubs Ukraine has led to a flourishing relationship that benefits the efforts of both organizations. HOPE's Ukraine program not only funds a portion of TC's annual budget, but it also opens doors for more children to hear the gospel.

Many parents hear of microfinance through their children's involvement in TC, and many children hear about TC through their parents' involvement with microfinance. It's this pairing—working capital with children's after-school programs—that has begun to reshape minds and transform lives.

Through one of these savings groups, Pastor Albert's family developed a growing burden for the local children and learned of TC. Connections like this have been instrumental in paving the way for the spread of TC throughout Ukraine. The club that opened in Pastor Albert's community quickly grew from fifteen to thirty youths. That club now serves as a bridge between the church and the community, allowing many community members to learn about God through their children's involvement with TC.

According to Maksym Slyvka, Tomorrow Clubs Marketing Director, "None of this would be possible if HOPE International did not start in Ukraine." As a result of a substantial partnership, and through the intentional curriculum set forth in the savings groups and loan meetings, kids have far greater exposure to a message that is changing lives forever.

Microfinance with Jesus in the Center

Christ-centered microfinance has a more comprehensive, holistic approach than secular microfinance. With an understanding of the holistic nature of poverty, Christ-centered microfinance takes into account more than just the material lack of poverty. It recognizes that poverty affects every part of the human experience, influencing relationships with family and community, perceptions and interactions with God, self-esteem and self-confidence, and more.

A Christ-centered approach boldly introduces participants to Jesus, to biblical principles for work and life, to local pastors, to Scripture and to prayer. It creates community as participants take out loans or save money in groups. A beautiful synergy occurs as participants regularly meet together, cheer each other on, and support one another's businesses.

Though individuals of any religious background or affiliation can join, loan meetings and savings group meetings can look quite similar to a church small group or life group, with the addition of financial accountability.[22]

Many members bring their children to these meetings to play with other children as the meeting goes on. Younger children sit on the laps of their moms or of their mom's friends, dancing during worship and closing their eyes during prayer. Older children sometimes sit in the back, listening in and learning through observation. It's often a family affair, and people's lives inevitably move toward God.[23]

The bottom line is this: Christ-centered microfinance helps individuals on their journey toward lasting life transformation and heart change. It aims to help the person enslaved by addiction to find freedom through relationship with Jesus. It helps to build the muscle of generosity by teaching people how to set up an emergency fund for themselves and for others in the community. Ultimately, it teaches individuals how to steward money and use it to provide a path forward out of the grip of extreme poverty in a way that honors God, re-establishes dignity, and blesses others.

As a result, kids' lives are changed. As parents grow in their relationship with Jesus, they introduce Him to their children and teach them biblical truths. Their associations shift and habits change; they begin to spend more time with people in their community who share similar values. Families begin attending church together and distance themselves from former unhealthy relationships. As parents pray, children learn to pray. The trickle-down effect is transformational and lasting because the groups continue to meet, save, grow, and invest. Hearts change and the message of the gospel spreads. Small, independent economies and faith communities are birthed and nurtured, creating opportunity and hope where none existed. And who wins? Kids do—and in a big way.

Kids Win with
Spiritual Growth

Only a holistic approach that addresses material, personal, social, and spiritual transformation can solve a problem as complex and deeply rooted as poverty. Christianity is the largest religion in the world, with 31.2 percent of the world's population identifying as Christians (2015).[24] Only 6 percent of microfinance clients worldwide, however, are served by a Christ-centered organization that cares for both material and spiritual needs.[25]

As parents get involved with Christ-centered organizations, their children are impacted for years to come. One study showed that children with religiously active parents are less affected later in life by childhood disadvantages than children whose parents were not as religiously active.[26]

Kids win with Spiritual Growth
through Christ-centered microfinance.

This story showed how kids win through
Christ-centered microfinance in these additional areas:

 Valuing Work   Improved Housing

 Thriving Families   Sufficient Food

 Sufficient Clothing   Basic Education

Chapter Six

Kids Win with Improved Housing

Francine the Ice Cream Lady

Despite its lush history, lovely weather, gorgeous mountains, and abundant natural resources, by the 1990s Haiti had become the poorest country in the Western Hemisphere. In 1996, when Francine was just sixteen years old, she and her family made the desperate, and yet courageous decision to leave Haiti and emigrate to the Dominican Republic. They were in search of work and a better life.

New Beginnings

A little over a decade after she arrived in the Dominican Republic, Francine found herself living in a rural part of Boca Chica that had unpaved roads and large, undeveloped spaces. She and her husband had three children: Frankli, Franchieli, and Maiki. Francine cared for her children in their tiny, tin-roofed home. Frankli was going to school, and life settled into the pattern Francine had always hoped for.

One day, Francine learned she was pregnant with her fourth child. The difficulty was, however, that her husband seemed to be pulling away. He didn't come home, and he began spending most of his earnings on himself instead of on Francine and the kids. Without much food, Francine worried that a lack of nutrition would compromise her pregnancy, perhaps even cause a miscarriage.

Would her husband come back? If not, how would she and her children survive? Francine felt overwhelmed with confusion and the daunting unknowns. How would she provide for herself and her baby, while keeping her other kids healthy?

While the questions kept coming, few answers arrived.

A Strange, Divine Dream

During her pregnancy, Francine had a vivid, powerful dream. She believed God spoke to her through it, reassuring her that she would be okay.

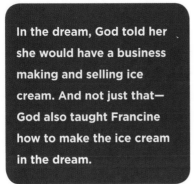

In the dream, God told her she would have a business making and selling ice cream. And not just that—God also taught Francine how to make the ice cream in the dream.

In the dream, God told her she would have a business making and selling ice cream. And not just that—God also taught Francine how to make the ice cream in the dream, even showing her what ingredients to use and the process needed to make it. For one flavor, she was to use coconut, cinnamon, sugar, and purified water. God showed her exactly how much of each ingredient to use for each flavor she was to make. The dream felt so *real* and so utterly different from any other dream she had ever had.

Through this dream, God gave Francine hope that she could find a path forward for herself and her children. Although she had no way to start a business at the time, every detail of the vivid dream remained emblazoned in her mind.

Painful Losses

Despite a difficult pregnancy, Francine soon gave birth to another son, Michael. Unfortunately, likely due to poor nutrition during the pregnancy, Michael was small and sick. And then, just six months after his birth, Michael died.

The tragedy pierced Francine's heart, bringing with it the familiar pangs of desperation and despair. Those emotions only intensified when her husband fully abandoned her and the other children, leaving her utterly alone. Although weighed down by loneliness, heartache, and grief, Francine resolved that, for herself and her children, she must be strong and find a path forward.

With options few and far between, the odds seemed stacked against Francine. She was an undocumented immigrant, who didn't speak Spanish, and had little education. She had no income and no job. Francine felt powerless, hopeless, and in great despair.

> **Dominican Republic**
>
> Although the Dominican Republic has seen strong economic growth in recent years, a large gap remains in the distribution of wealth.[1] The richest 10 percent of the population is mostly white descendants of Spanish settlers, who own most of the land and who benefit from 40 percent of national income. The residents living in the most extreme poverty are mostly of Haitian origin.[2]

A Ray of *Esperanza*

One day, a friend told Francine about an organization called Esperanza International, named after the Spanish word for "hope." The friend suggested that people from Esperanza were kind and might loan her some money.

Francine immediately remembered the dream God had given her about making and selling ice cream. Could this be the path toward that dream? Francine's friend said Esperanza would teach her how to use the loan wisely and help her new business to succeed. She would also have the opportunity to join a group of other women who would support each other in their businesses and lives.

> **Francine worried that Esperanza wouldn't want to lend to her. She wore old clothes, and she lacked the proper residency documents and citizenship papers. Why would anyone take a risk on someone like her?**

It sounded too good to be true. Francine worried that Esperanza wouldn't want to lend to her. Why would they? She wore old clothes, and she lacked the proper residency documents and citizenship papers. Why would anyone take a risk on someone like her?

Despite her doubts, Francine met with the loan officer from Esperanza. She learned that Esperanza required women to come together in a group and guarantee each other's loans: If one didn't repay, the others would have to pay it for them. Because of this rule, Francine took care to let only responsible women into her group. Once the group formed, the women immediately started to bond. They knew their success depended upon each other. They called themselves "Valientes," which means "The Brave Ones."

Much to Francine's delight, Esperanza loaned her 8,000 pesos ($160)— just enough to launch her into the ice cream business. With the loan, Francine bought a blender, a freezer, ingredients for ice cream, and plastic bags. Just as God had shown her, Francine prepared the mixture she had seen in her dream and then poured it into long, narrow plastic bags. She tied off each bag and lined them up in the freezer until they had turned into perfect,

single-serve ice cream treats. After they froze, Francine started walking the hot, dusty dirt roads and selling her ice cream treats for five pesos (10 cents) apiece.

By working hard and building up her business, Francine sold about 100 ice cream treats per day. At a 50 percent profit margin, she could make $5 per day—enough to make loan payments and feed her three children.

Returning to God

Before Francine got introduced to Esperanza, she had stopped going to church and described herself as spiritually "lukewarm." But as she continued to meet twice a month with the women in the loan group—praying, reading the Bible, and talking about loan repayments and running effective businesses—her attitude began to change.

As the women worshiped together, they grew closer to one another and to God. "God was calling me. He was coming after me," Francine remembered. After a long absence from church, Francine eventually started attending services again.

As Francine's spiritual life grew, so did her business. She hired her sister to help make the ice cream. She bought more coolers and employed young men to walk around town and sell her ice cream.

Three years after taking out her first loan, Francine used some of her profits to build a new cinder block house. What a step up from the old tin shack she had started with so many years prior! Sturdier and larger, it gave her family more space than ever before. What a great improvement for Francine and her three children!

In addition, Francine used the front half of the new home to run her business and to open a *colmado*. *Colmados*, common in the Dominican Republic, are little stores that often take up the front part of residential homes. They are used to sell items like filtered water, bread, coffee, charcoal, seasonal fruit, and more. In Francine's case, the "more" included ice cream! With this new combination of home and *colmado*, Francine became even better equipped to care for her children.

A Growing Business

Now, five years after taking out her first loan, Francine continues to run both the *colmado* and her ice cream business. She owns four freezers and several blenders. Her business employs her sister and three young men. Together, they make and sell about 400 ice cream treats a day which, after paying her workers, nets Francine $10-$12 each day. With her profits, she has enough to feed her children nutritious food, buy school uniforms and other clothing, and pay their tuition. She even pays a moto (motorcycle) taxi $10 a month to take her children to school.

By continuing to grow her business, Francine is empowered to provide for herself and her kids. She dreams that all three of her children will be able to study at the university, although she herself never had the opportunity. She plans to pay for their education, in part, by continuing to grow her business.

A Confident Entrepreneur

Francine has become a confident and capable entrepreneur. She continues to thank God for the ice cream dream He gave her. "I feel good about God because this is what He promised me."

She also praises God for the people of Esperanza, a group of men and women who took a chance on her and loaned her 8,000 pesos ($160) to help make her ice cream business become a reality. This loan empowered her to create and capitalize on the ice cream business, to own a little store, and to manage several employees. More than that, the loan helped her to put food on the table, fund a new home for her family, pave a path toward primary and secondary education for her kids, and bring her closer to Jesus. With the help of Christ-centered microfinance, Francine saw her dream come true.

Kids Win with
Improved Housing

The UN calls the right to adequate housing, including the right to live in a place with dignity and security, a basic human right. Yet, approximately 1.6 billion people lack access to safe and secure housing.[3]

More than 80 percent of the world's population lacks legal documentation of their property rights, increasing their vulnerability to displacement.[4] Lacking access to adequate housing has far-reaching consequences. It is estimated that 10 million people worldwide die each year from conditions related to substandard housing.[5]

Housing has a great impact on the entire family, especially on children. Studies show that children of homeowners are more likely to finish high school and are 59 percent more likely to become homeowners themselves.[6]

Kids win with Improved Housing through Christ-centered microfinance.

This story showed how kids win through
Christ-centered microfinance in these additional areas:

 Valuing Work

 Thriving Families

 Adequate Clothing

 Spiritual Growth

 Sufficient Food

Basic Education

Chapter Seven

Kids Win with Adequate Healthcare
I Just Put God First

Like many other villagers from Malawi, Bertha's parents were deeply committed to traditional religion. Witch doctors, ancestral worship, spiritism, and similar beliefs and practices shaped the way they lived. Therefore, when Bertha contracted a serious illness as a young child, her parents turned to traditional religion.

Bertha just got worse.

Her legs, arms, and abdomen swelled to the point that she could barely move. The inflammation seemed to cover her body like a blanket, getting hotter and tighter as the minutes ticked by. As the swelling grew, her body became contorted and stiff. No one in the village could diagnose the illness.

"This child is about to die," whispered villagers.

Bertha heard the dagger-like words, but she refused to believe them. Despite the swelling, she felt no pain.

Since the age of seven, Bertha had been cultivating a growing faith in God, much to the disapproval of her parents. In spite of her parent's refusal to allow her to attend a local church down the street, she continued to attend simply because she felt led to do so. It was as if a supernatural force let her know she needed to go. As a result of her growing childlike faith, she chose to cling to the hope that God would keep His promise to stay by her side and never leave her.

Unfortunately, Bertha's parents did not share their daughter's faith. Nor did they look fondly upon Christianity, insisting that she fully adopt their local traditions.

But Bertha loved to pray to God. She would often sneak away from her family to find comfort in solitude, conversing with the Lord. The intimacy she cultivated with God ultimately created the foundation for a firm faith that would help her make many crucial decisions later in life.

Despite the villagers' grim expectations, the illness did not kill Bertha. Yet her health problems didn't completely disappear, either. After some time, a family friend took her to Lilongwe, the capital of Malawi, in hopes of gaining a better life and a path toward healing. Over many weeks, Bertha's sickness abated and her body stopped swelling. God had brought her back to health, just as she had prayed.

Enjoying Work

As Bertha grew older, she worked as a housekeeper, a dishwasher, a nanny, and a cook. Eventually, as a young woman, she moved to Mzuzu, where she met her husband, Jairus Jemimba. The new couple moved back to her home village. They soon learned she was pregnant with their first child—and once more, Bertha's legs began to swell.

"This time around, she's going to die," the villagers insisted. They remembered Bertha's struggles as a child, and they knew the risks of pregnancy would only complicate her serious condition. Others predicted that her baby wouldn't survive the pregnancy.

Thoughts of death began creeping into Bertha's mind, and discouragement overshadowed her waking hours. But she chose to fight. Despite her poor health, she chose to cling to hope and faith, pushing through the discouragement that continued to encroach on her thoughts. She'd seen the Lord heal her before, and she stood on the hope that He would do so again.

"I have grown," she said. "I've witnessed everything that's happened in my life. I know what the hand of God can do in me."

And once more, God's hand did deliver her, despite her neighbors' gloomy prophecies. She gave birth to a beautiful, *healthy* baby girl. By the grace of God, Bertha and Jairus would eventually have a total of six children.

An Unspeakable Tragedy

One ordinary evening, as the wind blew softly across the night sky, the kids played quietly in the spacious but bare living room beneath the straw roof. When bedtime came, the children found their place on the blue tarp spread across the dirt floor and nestled against each other. Bertha's mother was staying with their family at the time, and she joined the kids as they cuddled

> ## Malawi
> Although Malawi has made significant economic and structural reforms in the past decade, it remains one of the poorest countries on the planet, with a GDP per capita of $338.48 (2017).[1] Malawi ranks 171 out of 189 on the Human Development Index (2017).[2] Around 53 percent of Malawi's population lives below the poverty line of $1.90 a day, which makes access to healthcare challenging. Half of Malawi's population of 18 million must travel one hour to get to the nearest community health center, and two-and-a-half hours to get to a hospital.[3]

together and quieted their minds and mouths in preparation for the night. One by one, they drifted off to sleep.

Without warning, a scream pierced the darkness. Bertha shot upright on her tarp, adrenaline coursing through her veins. "What happened, mother?" she called out in the darkness. She didn't wait for an answer. Grim stares and tear-filled eyes met her as she darted into the other room. Her children and her mother had gathered around the second oldest, Isaac,[1] who lay still on the ground, his eyes wide open, unflinching and unblinking.

---

[1] This name has been changed for privacy purposes.

They shook him and shouted his name, desperately hoping his body would move and that breath would return to his lungs. But his stiff body grew cold, and they realized he had died.

The shock and trauma shook the family, especially since they had no idea why he had died. Bertha's inconsolable pain felt like a bottomless cavern, but she had to find the strength to press on. She needed to help provide for her family—and it would take a boost of faith to get her through this heartbreaking loss.

Financial Assistance Through Community

As Bertha and Jairus tried to pick up the pieces after their son's sudden death, they had a tough time making ends meet. To generate additional income, Bertha began running a small business selling tomatoes, grass, and pumpkins.

While her efforts helped the family get by, Bertha did not make enough money to handle unforeseen troubles, such as illnesses and medical bills. When life got really tough, the family had two responses: to pray, and to hope that others would respond generously to their plight.

One warm autumn afternoon, Bertha returned home from selling crops in Kauma, a small village in Malawi. When she arrived home, a concerned neighbor exclaimed, "Your son has been very sick! He fainted!"

Bertha rushed inside to see her twelve-year-old son, Abel. She flung herself down by his side, noticing his bloodshot eyes and feeling his overly-warm body. He struggled to breathe.

Her mind began to churn. *We have no money to take him to the hospital,* she thought. Remembering that the pastor's wife lived nearby, Bertha called for her believing friend to come and pray over her son. As the pair prayed, Abel's breathing slowly began to improve.

A few days later, Bertha took Abel to a public hospital, where he tested positive for tuberculosis. There, she got free medicine for their son, and he began to recover. Knowing that Abel still had a long recovery ahead of him, Bertha felt overwhelmed with the impending healthcare costs. She didn't know if they'd be able to afford it.

One day, however, everything changed.

At church, Bertha heard an announcement that the following week any interested parties could hear about a new initiative called "savings groups." The news intrigued Bertha, along with many others in the congregation.

The next week, Bertha and the others learned how these savings groups worked. Participants would pool their money together and save it in a secure place. They could even loan each other money, which they would then repay over time at an interest rate set by their own group. Working together in community, they could steadily build their savings, building a buffer to use when emergencies, life events, and other needs arose.

> As Bertha reflected on her family's challenges with money—specifically, the difficulty they had with saving—she fell in love with the idea of accountability and with the possibility of taking out a loan one day. She could hardly wait to get started.

As Bertha reflected on her family's challenges with money—specifically, the difficulty they had with saving—she fell in love with the idea of accountability and with the possibility of taking out a loan one day. She could hardly wait to get started.

A Quiet Hope

While Jairus continued with his own work, Bertha quietly held onto the hope of one day owning a shop. In the meantime, she determined to work hard to grow her tomato business. At the very least, she knew she could depend on the encouragement and support of her fellow group members, people she trusted to help her succeed in both life and faith.

Joining a savings group drastically changed Bertha's life and the lives of her children. The group had come to feel like family to her, supporting her in countless ways. Group members prayed for each other, supported each other's businesses, and united together in difficult situations.

The savings group also had a huge impact on the health of her family and on their ability to afford medical care in times of need. "Since I joined the group," she said, "we're healthy. Our health is progressing."

And it's not just her physical health that's seen a change; many facets of Bertha's life look very different today than they once did. Since joining the group, she says, "I've noticed a big difference in my house. I have clothes to wear. I have food to feed my family. I have enough clothes for my children. I've hired people who are farming my land. I've witnessed a lot of things improving. Even here, people who have surrounded me can see a lot of things improving.

> "Before, I would just spend the money somehow. I didn't know how to save money properly. But right now, I'm able to save the money. I'm able to invest in something big that benefits my family in the end."

"This group has opened my mind. I'm able to save money. Before, I could accumulate money, but I would just buy irrelevant things for the kids to eat; I would just spend the money somehow. I didn't know how to utilize the money properly. I didn't know how to save money properly. But right now, I'm able to save the money. I'm able to invest in something big that benefits my family in the end."

A Strong Faith

Bertha's faith has grown strong and continues to grow stronger. "The more I hear the Word of God preached in that church," she said, "the more I get encouraged. The more I continue to stand strong, the more I know that God is not going to leave me. I cannot feel okay when I'm not praying. I just kneel down, and I know that God is in control."

Despite her struggles with sickness and the deaths of beloved family members, Bertha speaks with confidence. "I just put God first. I knew that God had a purpose for those kids. I can say now that I *feel* good. I know that it's weird to say that, but I feel God. Everything that I do, I put it in God's hands. I kneel down and put God first. And every time, God has come through."

Before she had the opportunity to join a savings group, confronting sickness or health challenges continually left Bertha feeling vulnerable— she had no way to see it coming and no idea what would happen. Gaining the ability to reliably save money gave both Bertha and Jairus peace of mind, knowing their kids would have what they needed if something unforeseeable should happen. Jairus says, "I feel really great knowing that my wife is in the savings group... It helps my family."

Bertha's story paints a picture of extreme poverty. It was as if her family was standing at a cliff's edge, with their toes dangling over it, holding their breath and hoping a gust of wind wouldn't push them over. The opportunity to save was like taking several steps away from the brink, pulling them back toward safety. Life felt safer, steadier, and less volatile. Bertha now has a vision and a means to provide for her children in ways she never had before.

Bertha's savings group, coupled with continually putting God first, enabled her to have a clear, attainable path toward sufficient food, clothing, and healthcare for her family.

Kids Win with
Adequate Healthcare

Less than half of the world's population receives the health services it needs, often because individuals cannot afford the cost.[4] In 2010, almost 100 million people landed in extreme poverty as a result of paying for health services out of their own pockets.[5]

Dire situations presented by pandemics like COVID-19 most adversely impact those in extreme poverty, as well. With limited access to healthcare, less doctors and practitioners per capita in rural areas, and the economic impact on small businesses, those in poverty struggle to obtain the services and finances they need.[6] Inadequate access to healthcare has a significant impact on the lives of children. It is estimated that spending $1 billion in expanding immunization coverage against preventable diseases could save the lives of 1 million children each year.[7] Children born into poverty are almost twice as likely to die before the age of five as children from wealthier families.[8] In the past decade, improvements in health and healthcare led to a 24 percent increase in income in some of the world's poorest countries.[9]

Kids win with Adequate Healthcare through Christ-centered microfinance.

This story showed how kids win through
Christ-centered microfinance in these additional areas:

	Thriving Families		Spiritual Growth
	Sufficient Clothing		Sufficient Food

Chapter Eight

Kids Win with Sufficient Food
Sink and Rise

The three sandbars of Lu-li Island seem to wade in the sea during low tide, their golden ridges resting in the crystal blue water until the high tide smothers their peaks. Travelers have stood on these sandbars for years, admiring how the landmarks appear to sink and rise with the ocean.

One might think of it as ocean-view poetry, so inspiring the island derives its name from the sinking-rising illusion: "Lu-li" comes from the Philippine language Tagalog words *lulubog* and *lilitaw*, which mean sinking and rising. The name is symbolic: The two words mirror the Philippines' scar-pocked history, a history marked by intense challenges to rise and build a better future.

10 Million Women in Poverty

After 350 years and 300 rebellions, the Philippines successfully won independence from Spanish colonial rule in 1898.[1] But challenges continued. Various regimes followed two peaceful revolutions, spearheaded by citizens attempting to build a better government safe from corrupt rulers.

While the Philippines boasts rich natural resources and many of its citizens have risen out of poverty along with the nation's growing economy, social and economic inequities remain high. Around 26.5 percent of the population, including 10 million women, still live below the poverty line.[2]

Annalyn Estrella, mother of four, once numbered herself among those 10 million women. She lost nearly all of her assets when she put everything she had toward helping her bedridden mother stay alive. Although she describes life in the Philippines as painfully challenging, Annalyn explains these difficult seasons with the term *lulubog-lilitaw*—again, sinking and rising.

> Annalyn Estrella, mother of four, lost nearly all of her assets when she put everything she had toward helping her bedridden mother stay alive.

Amid the pain of losing so much and feeling the unrelenting pressure of providing for her children, Annalyn saw hidden beauty during this challenging time. The support of a microfinance loan from the Center for Community Transformation (CCT) brought a high tide into her life that lifted her entire family. But her story starts about sixteen years earlier.

Snarling Doubts and Fears

Annalyn sprinkled flour onto the table's surface and began kneading dough, careful not to apply too much pressure along the table's edge. Annalyn's husband, Rolando, who sometimes worked in her bakery business, stood beside her, hip to hip, massaging the ingredients with large, calloused hands. They couldn't risk a wobble, for the noise might disturb their three children, slumbering beneath the rickety table. Their home, all ten by thirteen feet of it, included a small kitchen and tight sleeping areas. Although they lived modestly, Annalyn was grateful for the bakery business.

One day, Annalyn's mother's skin grew pale, her eyes twitched, and then, with little warning, her legs buckled. She crumpled to the floor, unconscious.

Annalyn rushed her mother to the hospital, where medical staff confined her to the Intensive Care Unit for a month. The nurses told Annalyn that her mother had suffered a stroke. Little did Annalyn know that her mother would remain bedridden for the next ten years.

In the three years that followed, almost all of their income supported Annalyn's mother's medical expenses. No longer able to pay the bakery's bills, they lost all of their property. Even their electricity and water got cut off. Without these utilities, Annalyn worried for her family's safety and health. She sold almost all of her belongings, including her vehicle and their house in Bulacan. She kept only her baking equipment. Unable to pay her employees, Annalyn lost her production helpers, bakers, and sales people.

Philippines

The Philippines boasts abundant natural resources, and many of its citizens have risen out of poverty with the nation's growing economy—a GDP per capita of nearly $3,000 (2017).[3] Although the Philippines has seen significant economic advancements, social and economic inequities remain high, especially in rural areas.

The Philippines has a Human Development Index ranking of 113 out of 189 countries.[4] Approximately 26.5 percent of the population lives below the poverty line of $1.90 a day.[5] And 7 million Filipinos live in ultrapoverty, living on less than 50 cents a day, with 22 percent of them going to bed hungry at least once a week.[6]

She felt a piercing sorrow in her heart when they could no longer afford basic meals for their children. In the morning, she would set out very small plates of *viand* (a meat, seafood, or vegetable dish that accompanies rice in a Filipino meal) made with *galungong* (a common, inexpensive fish in the Philippines). Typically, her family of six shared four pieces of fish per meal, twice a day. When bedtime came, her children often crawled into their sleeping area, while Annalyn listened to their empty stomachs growling with hunger.

Her daughter, Karina, recalls how desperately she craved different fruits and vegetables. She remembers how they "sacrificed everything just to keep [their] grandmother alive." Karina adds, "At that time we didn't know Christ yet, so we didn't know who to call or depend on. We felt that was the end of the rope, and we had no chance to rise up from that pitiful situation and improve our living conditions."

> Before Annalyn's mother got sick, they had plenty of friends in the community. But after they lost almost all of their assets and their business went into bankruptcy, many of these friends acted as if they didn't know Annalyn or her family anymore.

Annalyn said she felt as though she had dropped to zero. "I almost gave up," she admitted. "I didn't want to go back to business anymore." If only she could turn back time! Before Annalyn's mother got sick, they had plenty of friends in the community. But after they lost almost all of their assets and their business went into bankruptcy, many of these friends acted as if they didn't know Annalyn or her family anymore. Karina remembers that "for every help they extended to us, we also received *sumbat* (scolding or reproach)."

After losing almost all of their belongings, Annalyn had only one dream: that her four children might have enough food and could finish their studies. She couldn't imagine any other inheritance to pass on to them.

Although Annalyn always had an interest in and love for business, she recalls feeling aimless. "I was doing the bakery business, but there was no direction and no determination. Because in the first place, I was living far from our Lord. I didn't know Him yet."

Annalyn debated whether she should give up her passion for her bakery business and return home to Masbate province, in the Bicol region, and just plant *kamote* (sweet potato). She laughs now, remembering how at that time she "tried to make bread, but it was hard as wood. Yes, I operated a bakery before, but I didn't know how to make bread myself. Terrible!"

A Hand Up, Not a Handout

Thankfully, Annalyn's neighbors saw her struggles and reached out to her. Annalyn remembers how "they pitied me because I couldn't even buy an adult diaper for my bedridden mother." Members of CCT encouraged Annalyn to take out a small loan to invest in her business.

After losing almost everything she owned, however, Annalyn felt hesitant to borrow money. She worried that she wouldn't be able to pay it back. Not only that, but the program required participants to save PHP 50 (97 cents) every week, an amount she thought she could better use for other basic needs. On top of everything, she felt concerned about committing time to attend CCT's fellowship meetings and Bible studies. She thought only of the time it would snatch from her endless house chores and business efforts.

Annalyn's neighbors persisted anyway, despite her concerns and hesitations. They believed that a loan of PHP 4,000 ($78) could help her start anew.

Finally, one Tuesday morning, Annalyn peeked in to overhear a CCT fellowship meeting. Ashamed to be seen out in public, she lingered near the door. As she leaned in to listen, she got bumped and fell forward into the room. Embarrassed to leave, she stayed. During the meeting, she could think only of her empty store, until she heard the pastor speak a life-changing verse:

"Come to me, all you who are weary and heavy burdened,
and I will give you rest."
(Matthew 11:28)

Annalyn recalls the moment with crystal clarity: "It really struck me and touched my heart. I almost forgot that there's God. Why had I carried all my burdens all by myself? There's still God. Why didn't I ask for help from Him?"

Annalyn recalls the moment with crystal clarity: "It really struck me and touched my heart. I almost forgot that there's God. Why had I carried all my burdens all by myself? There's still God. Why didn't I ask for help from Him?"

After the meeting, the pastor handed Annalyn a small New Testament, which she hid under her armpit while walking home. Despite feelings of shame and hesitation, she continually read that small Bible whenever she caught a moment of rest at home.

Something Changed Within

As Annalyn's heart opened, she agreed to join CCT. Her neighbor helped her to secure all of the necessary requirements, like a residence certificate and identification, to get her first loan.

Annalyn remembers how something had changed within her: "To my mind, money was no longer important. Instead, I was very excited to hear the pastor's message and verses from the Bible. I liked the prayers. Every Tuesday, I waited for the pastor to pass along the road so I could ask him a lot of questions and accompany him early to the fellowship venue. Our fellowship meeting was at 9 a.m., but I was already there by 7:30 a.m. It was one-on-one discipleship, and subsequently, I was born again."

In that way, Annalyn took the first step toward revitalizing her life.

Through CCT's step-by-step plan, Annalyn learned how to responsibly manage her money. As she gained the trust of CCT staff by diligently paying back her loans, she was able to take out larger ones. This allowed her to rebuild her bakery business and grow her profits. She became motivated to "really level up" her business by finding a wider market for her products.

She began hiring workers, providing opportunities for many members of her community. She also bought a plot of land in Masbate and opened a branch of her bakery in the Batangas province.

Extended Blessings

Annalyn has far surpassed the dream she once considered impossible. Her children have enrolled in private school, and her eldest won a scholarship. Three of her older children have already graduated from college.

Karina remembers how she once could barely study in the family's tight, overcrowded home. She recalls fearing that their circumstances would never change. "I'm really proud that I have finished my college degree," she declares, "with the help of CCT." She earned her Bachelor of Science degree in Business Administration and Human Resource Development Management.

Although friends tell Annlyn that she can rest now that her children have gone to school and are stable, she says she hopes to continue to maximize the capabilities and opportunities that God offers her. She dreams of expanding her business with her children, so they can manage it in the future or even become leaders in their own businesses. Business unites her family, she insists. When her husband or children return home from work or school, they talk excitedly about business and regularly support and encourage each other.

The loans from CCT have not only enhanced Annalyn's life, but also shaped her children's work ethic and expanded their hope for the future. "If we hadn't known CCT," Karina says, "perhaps we wouldn't have known what kind of life there was ahead of us. Aside from providing us loans for additional capital, CCT also taught us how to manage

> The loans from CCT have not only enhanced Annalyn's life, but also shaped her children's work ethic and expanded their hope for the future. "If we hadn't known CCT," Karina says, "perhaps we wouldn't have known what kind of life there was ahead of us."

our business properly through seminars, training, and mentoring. Most importantly, we have gotten to know God through CCT. Now, if we face life challenges, we are not easily depressed because we have God, with whom we can share all our burdens. Life is easy because God is there to support and guide us, always. He knows all the best for His children. That's why we always put our trust in Him."

Rising

While Annalyn's family once ate the same meal twice a day, they now eat a balanced diet of fruits, vegetables, and meat. Annalyn says that today, whenever her family gets hungry or wants something to eat, they can buy whatever they need. They live in a clean, two-story building with six bedrooms, a bakery, and a store. She's saving to buy the building. She also owns a six-unit apartment building, which she rents out.

Not so long ago, Annalyn felt as though she were living without direction or purpose. She felt her family was sinking more than rising. But today, beyond all question, they are rising.

Kids Win with
Sufficient Food

More than 800 million people worldwide suffer from hunger.[7] The number of those going hungry has increased since 2014— a troubling fact, as hunger impacts our economies, health, education, equality, and social development.[8] Hunger and malnutrition can hinder physical growth, reduce productivity, and increase susceptibility to illnesses, making it more difficult for people to improve their livelihoods and creating a barrier to sustainable development.

Poor nutrition has a devastating effect on children, claiming the lives of 3.1 million kids each year. In fact, malnutrition can be attributed to nearly half of the deaths of children who die before the age of five.[9]

Kids win with Sufficient Food
through Christ-centered microfinance.

This story showed how kids win through
Christ-centered microfinance in these additional areas:

 Valuing Work

 Improved Housing

 Thriving Families

Basic Education

 Spiritual Growth

Chapter Nine

Kids Win with Basic Education
How Much Is a Dream Worth?

How much is a dream worth? Or, perhaps better, how much does a dream cost?

We all have dreams. For a child living in extreme poverty, however, limited resources can prevent dreams from becoming reality. More than 25 percent of Ethiopia's 109 million citizens live below the poverty line, making it one of the most impoverished countries in the world.[1]

Photo: Destiny Academy

With a literacy rate hovering around 50 percent and a relatively high rate of unemployment, millions of Ethiopians labor every day merely to stay alive. How can they feed their dreams, too?

Haregewin (Hareg) Geresu knows what it's like to dream and to invest in the dreams of others. When Hareg and her husband, Yonatan, moved to Addis Ababa, Ethiopia, in 2004, she heard a woman describe a Christian school, a concept she didn't know existed in Addis Ababa. She had always loved kids and knew she would do something to help them—perhaps she could run a school? But how?

"Where would we get the money?" she asked herself. "How much would it take? We don't even know how much we need." Nevertheless, the couple birthed a dream of creating a high-quality, low-cost school for children who might not otherwise be able to afford it. Would it work? They intended to find out.

Building Destiny

Hareg and Yonatan founded Destiny Academy in 2005, and the school now serves about 500 students on two campuses. One campus hosts almost 150 kindergarteners, divided into three classes (ages three to four, four to five, and five to six), while the second campus educates about 350 students from first to eighth grade. The school accepts students of all religious backgrounds. Destiny's staff is largely Christian and Hareg, who manages the day to day operations of the school, infuses a Christian perspective into everything the school does. The Ethiopian government does not allow explicitly "Christian" schools, so Hareg states they have committed to "instill[ing] our values in the teachings, in the administrative staff, in our extracurricular activities."

Hareg instills Destiny's values into each of the school's lesson plans. "We usually start with respect and love," she said. "We take those values and repeatedly integrate them into our lessons. We also do prayer time in the morning, at lunch time, and at snack time. If parents ask, we tell them that this is not about religion; we want our students to be grateful for what they have."

DESTINY ACADEMY

Photo: Destiny Academy

The rented facilities of her brightly colored school lie in the heart of Addis Ababa. The school logo features a yellow crest with a "D" in the center and an arrow pointing to the right, inspired by the words of Psalm 127:4: "Like arrows in the hands of a mighty warrior are children born in one's youth."

Painted numbers and letters as well as pictures of animals adorn the walls of the school's courtyard. Photos of past students, several of them in graduation gear, line other walls. It doesn't take long to realize that Hareg is well-loved: Students in black-and-orange uniforms swarm Hareg, throwing their arms around her and planting kisses on her cheeks.

"I remember coming here when it was very different," Hareg recalls. She points to a street and says, "This road was not even here, even though people have been living here a long time. We chose this area because it's very needy. A lot of families needed support. Even today, there aren't a lot of schools able to provide quality education."

The Growth of Destiny

Back in 2004, a family friend who worked at a private college offered to give Hareg and Yonatan a small amount of seed money to start their school. They wouldn't have been able to get started without it. After the couple created a budget, Hareg left her job and their friend gave them half of what he'd promised, intending to give them the other 50 percent as a shareholder when the school grew.

"We rented this place and paid for six months," Hareg said. "The first day, I just had a table and a chair. I was crying. I didn't know what to do." Not long afterward, the family friend disappeared without providing the

Ethiopia

Ethiopia, the second most populous nation in Africa, has a population of approximately 109 million (2018). It also has the fastest growing economy in the region.[2]

The World Bank calls Ethiopia one of the most educationally disadvantaged countries in the world. This is due to armed conflict, famines, and humanitarian crises.[3] Many schools in Ethiopia also lack basic facilities and resources, especially in rural areas. More than 75 percent of elementary schools do not have access to electricity (2015).[4]

second half of the funds. His other business had gone bankrupt. Despite never receiving the remainder of the funds, Hareg plowed ahead with her vision for Destiny Academy.

When Destiny began in 2005, it had only three students. Hareg established kindergarten first, followed by another grade each year thereafter. Although public schools are free in Ethiopia, typical classrooms overflow with fifty to sixty students, and the level of instruction can lack consistency and excellence.

"It is amazing," Hareg remembers. "God knew how we could start it. I have a lot of crazy stories. For me, looking back gives me strength to go forward. It is good to remember what God has done."

Destiny Academy employs thirty-six teachers and sixty-five workers. It costs students $25 a month to attend, compared to eight to ten times that amount charged by other private schools. This year, eighteen Destiny students received scholarships to continue attending the school.

> "Education is not only about going to college; it is about giving perspective and confidence. Confidence can be an education. We want them to say, 'I can do this.'"

In addition to finding help with tuition, Destiny also assists its students with other household needs. "Especially in Africa, we have a responsibility to help single moms," Hareg declared. "It is our responsibility to bring food. I focus on the girls and on their education. I want them to learn how to stand by themselves, so that by age seventeen or eighteen, they know what to do and will not have to depend on a man. I have some really strong girls. Education is not only about going to college; it is about giving perspective and confidence. Confidence can be an education. We want them to say, 'I can do this.'"

One Child at a Time

Over the years, Hareg and Yonatan have brought several students into their own home when they've needed a place to stay. In the past year, for example, the parents of three students died, leaving them orphans with very little means to survive. "I would never charge them," Hareg said. "I could not in my heart make them pay."

Hareg has the opportunity to interact with students from all different walks of life. Frehiwot (Fre), a 15-year-old Destiny student, explained matter-of-factly, "I was raped when I was five years old. My mom brought us here to Addis so we could go to church and have holy baptism and communion … I kept insisting I wanted to go to school, but she kept me at home. She would go out on the street and beg."

One day, a woman found Fre on the street and suggested she be adopted. A government-run orphanage took her in but didn't send her to school for a year. She didn't stay long, because her mom returned one day with the news that she had found Fre's father. "She said she wanted to take me to him. I was so happy that they had found my dad."

But the man took her to the countryside and started to treat Fre like his wife. She described, "He said, 'You look like your mom,' and he tried to have a sexual relationship with me. After three weeks, I ran away." It turned out that the man was *not* her father after all.

Shortly after this incident, Hareg found out about Fre and started praying about what she might do to give her the opportunity to attend school at Destiny. Reflecting back, Hareg told Fre, "You know I didn't have anything. I did not have any money to support you. I prayed, 'Lord, if you want me to support her, I want to offer my heart.' I called Elsa (the woman who eventually adopted Fre) and told her to start looking for housing. I knew Elsa had only a modest income. This is one of the stories that really keeps me going."

In fact, Elsa did not at first think of adopting Fre. "That was not our first option," Elsa explained. "We were trying to arrange for her to stay with another family. The place we were living was tiny. Where would she stay? Where would she sleep? But I knew that even though I didn't have a place for her to sleep, God would provide. I could share the same food my son and I were eating. I was struggling, but I told myself over and over, 'I can do this.' I prayed hard. I prayed that I could be a good mom again." Soon enough, the adoption was finalized and Fre was formally a part of Elsa's family.

A Future Through Destiny

After Fre started attending school at Destiny, her outlook on life began to change. "When I go back and think of my past history, and then I think about today, I am very much joyful and happy," she said. "I was hopeless and did not have any hope. This is my hope. And I see the hope. Right now I have a really great life and am okay."

Fre is now in ninth grade biology, and she wants to become a doctor when she grows up. Confident her future will be beautiful, she declares, "With the family I have now, we plan together. We talk about what we are going to do. I am sure we are going to meet our goal."

Fre says she came to know God by observing her adopted family. "People around me have compassion. Watching their love and patience made me want to hear. God brought me to this specific place. He had a reason to bring me here. I had heard something about Jesus before, but people told me the wrong way. Now I know that I have found the right way."

Help for Nurturing Dreams

Photo: Destiny Academy

Fre and hundreds like her enjoy the chance to get a good education and nurture their dreams at good schools, in part because of groups like Edify. Edify works in eleven countries around the world, providing training, loan capital, and education technology to entrepreneurs providing Christ-centered education in their communities. The organization focuses its efforts predominantly in Latin America, Africa, and Asia. It provides resources to help effective, low-cost schools thrive. In Ethiopia alone, Edify has provided twenty-one microfinance loans to nineteen schools, amounting to more than half a million dollars.

> In Ethiopia alone, Edify has provided twenty-one microfinance loans to nineteen schools, amounting to more than half a million dollars.

Hareg first learned of Edify in 2014. Some of the organization's leaders had come to Ethiopia to "scout out" the educational landscape and learned of seventeen schools with Christian roots. Almost immediately, the group connected school leaders with one another to help them build a sense of solidarity.

The next year, in 2015, Destiny Academy took out a $20,000 loan from Edify to make classroom and playground improvements. The school finished repaying the loan in December 2017. Yonatan has also continued to support the school and now works as the country director for Edify in Ethiopia.

In the future, Hareg says she would like to take out a larger loan to buy land for the school, as it currently rents its facilities. She says Destiny Academy could also use funds to buy computers and more books.

A Vision to Help

How much will dreams cost? Because of microfinance loans, influencers like Hareg and Yonatan have the opportunity to sow into the lives of local children. They weave together the fabric of their culture, one child at a time, with proper education and care. As they plant seeds of vision, hope, and restoration in the hearts of the children entrusted to them, they play an incredibly significant role in the lives of Ethiopia's next generation of leaders.

"God will give you a vision," Hareg tells her students. "A vision to help others, to reach out to other people. Imagine if you become a doctor and try to help a mom and daughter! God will give you that vision. You will start to believe."

As Hareg considers the work that she and her colleagues do, she declares, "This is our encouragement in life, to say 'yes' to these students. Yes, it is very hard! But the Lord is good, no matter what."

Photo: Destiny Academy

Kids Win with

Basic Education

Although enrollment in primary education in developing countries has reached 91 percent, 57 million children still do not have the opportunity to attend school.[5] More than half of these children live in sub-Saharan Africa.[6] Global estimates claim that approximately 617 million children of primary and lower secondary school age lack minimum proficiency in reading and mathematics.[7]

Education is crucial for upward socioeconomic mobility and provides opportunities for children to break from the cycle of poverty.[8] Education also helps to increase gender equality, improve health, and increase tolerance between societies.[9]

Kids win with Basic Education through Christ-centered microfinance.

This story showed how kids win through
Christ-centered microfinance in these additional areas:

 Valuing Work

 Spiritual Growth

Chapter Ten

Kids Win with Freedom from Trafficking

Better a Slave than Free?

With human trafficking, corrupt politics, and bleak economic conditions, much of Moldova's population has become vulnerable to exploitation.[1]

Moldova lies in the heart of a region in Eastern Europe known for its high levels of human trafficking. According to the International Organization for Migration, more than 300,000 Moldovans have been trafficked over the last twenty-five years.[2]

Photo: Beginning of Life

As trafficking has become a global crisis, with countless organizations joining together to fight it, perpetrators have developed their own innovative solutions to continue scaling up their efforts. Trafficking is a multifaceted, complex issue that takes various forms across the globe, but in Moldova, as in other parts of Eastern Europe, it has progressed in distinct stages.

A Morphing Disease

The first phase (late 1990s until the early 2000s) took the form depicted in the movie *Taken* and was marked by kidnappings (and with a reportedly significant role played by the mafia). Traffickers took victims from their homes, put them in car trunks, and deprived them of their identification.

In 2000, the United Nations General Assembly adopted the "Protocol to Prevent, Suppress and Punish Trafficking in Persons, Especially Women and Children," bringing global awareness to the problem.[3] The criminal practice received formal acknowledgment and was officially defined by the United Nations.[4]

The second phase of trafficking began to take form when criminal rings reacted to the global awakening and began to innovate. This was done by forming recruitment companies that provided job contracts to vulnerable individuals. Both the contract and the business were real, requiring victims to leave their country and move to the destination country in hopes of landing a job with better pay. Once they arrived in the new country, however, they were forced into trafficking.

Local law enforcement and humanitarian groups have steadily cracked down on these criminal efforts, and pimps and their accomplices have developed increasingly creative methods. More recently, criminal rings have become even more nuanced and discreet by provoking victims to think that selling themselves into slavery was their idea. It often looks something like what happened to Daria[l], whose story is captured below and based on true events.

Daria's Story

As a blossoming young adult, Daria sought to find a job that would help her to support herself and her family. With minimal employment opportunities in Moldova, Daria looked outside her home country. Soon, she received an official, legal contract for a new job in Italy, washing dishes for ten hours a day. The job would pay 600 euros a month. Since 600 euros was likely double or triple what she could earn in Moldova, she

l   This name has been changed for privacy purposes.

eagerly accepted. She felt confident she could live off of 200 euros a month and send the remaining 400 euros home to her family.

The recruiting company offered to pay for Daria's flight and registration and help her with housing arrangements. Upon her arrival in Italy, she moved into an apartment where several other girls already lived.

She immediately began her work at the restaurant, but within a few weeks, she realized that 600 euros fell far short of what she needed. No one had explained that she would have to pay for medical insurance, food, taxes, and other miscellaneous expenses. She needed all 600 euros (and more) to pay for her own immediate needs.

In addition to being fined for broken dishes and other mistakes she made on the job, Daria learned that the money for her flight and registration was a loan, not a gift, from the recruiting company. And the business owners were hungry for their money.

At first, Daria didn't know much about her roommates, other than they looked well-dressed, well-fed, and often drunk. She quickly learned that they worked as prostitutes. Daria couldn't imagine giving herself to such employment. But as she returned to her job day after day, she felt continually crushed by the harsh work environment and burdensome payments she had to make. Feeling trapped, she asked her roommates to introduce her to their employer.

> **Moldova**
>
> Moldova, once a wealthy and flourishing nation, is now the poorest country in Europe, with a GDP per capita of $2,724 (2018) and a Human Development Index ranking of 112 out of 189 countries (2017).[5]
>
> After the fall of the Soviet Union in the early 1990s, the economy plummeted. With limited opportunities, 16.5 percent of Moldova's working-age population searched for opportunities outside of the country, putting them at high risk for trafficking and exploitation in the process.[6]

It turned out she had already met him: Her manager owned the brothel that operated behind the restaurant. And when she asked for a job in the brothel, he obliged.

Just as he'd planned.

Daria knew she couldn't get the law involved. The owner remained above legal reproach because he didn't "force" her into prostitution, after all. She was the one who chose to approach her roommates and ask for the job.

Besides, even if she thought what was going on was wrong and should be reported to authorities back home, many Moldovan law enforcement officers have connections to (or are actively involved with) criminal rings.[7]

Resigning herself to this lifestyle in order to make ends meet and seeing no way out, Daria doubled down. Not only did she prostitute herself, she agreed to help recruit—a great way to earn some extra money.

As is often the case for victims of trafficking, Daria became a victim and a criminal at the same time. Following the blueprint of her own recruiters, she utilized her closest social circle—relatives, friends, local villagers—promising them wonderful opportunities outside of Moldova. Given the strong trust in her relationships, Daria had no trouble finding recruits. She just didn't give them the full story. Instead, she relied on the system. They would fall victim to the same cycle she had and would find themselves asking for "different" work soon enough.

> Daria became a victim and a criminal at the same time. Following the blueprint of her own recruiters, she utilized her closest social circle—relatives, friends, local villagers—promising them wonderful opportunities outside of Moldova.

Hard Times in Moldova

One victim trafficked from Moldova depressingly notes: "It is much better to be a slave in Europe than to be a free person in Moldova."

Like Daria, more than a quarter of Moldova's population has left the country to find work in other nations, hoping to earn enough money to send home a good portion of their earnings. This common practice leaves Moldova's economy largely dependent on remittances.

A 2014 census of Moldova showed its population at 2.9 million, down from 4.5 million at the beginning of the nineties. As a result of so much emigration, many children grow up without one or both parents and are raised instead by grandparents, aunts, and uncles.[8]

Why are Moldovans leaving by the masses? For one reason, corruption runs rampant, heightening the economic challenges citizens face. In 2014, $1 billion (the equivalent of one eighth of Moldova's GDP) was reportedly stolen through three banks and placed into the pockets of leading officials.[9] Furthermore, an opinion poll conducted by USAID in 2018 showed that only 16 percent of the population trust the justice of the Republic of Moldova.[10]

With a struggling economy and low trust in leadership, jobs are hard to come by and a sense of nationalism is virtually nonexistent. This makes options in other countries much more appealing.

From Exploitation to Dignity

Why do individuals become vulnerable to trafficking in all parts of the world, the U.S. included? Commonly, the cause can be traced to a serious lack of economic opportunity.[11] With a lack of money, a job, or an education, individuals can become at risk for exploitation and trafficking.

> With a lack of money, a job, or an education, individuals can become at risk for exploitation and trafficking.

Short-term thinking—survival thinking—can take over: *Why should I even think about saving for tomorrow, when the little I have could get taken away from me today?* Tremendous financial instability has led to intellectual, material, and emotional poverty. Deprived of innovative thinking by corrupt leaders who use their powers for their own gain, the general population slips toward a shortage of long-term thinking, innovation, and thoughtful leadership.

In cases like these, poverty can lead to trafficking. Trafficking is not the root issue, as many simply feel desperate to find opportunities for a better life.

This is where having opportunity makes a world of difference. Having access to a small amount of capital and having the chance to work with a loan officer who represents an organization that will boldly share the love of Jesus is a matter of life and death for some. Christ-centered microfinance not only provides a hand up to the local entrepreneur, but it keeps jobs in the country. It helps entrepreneurs build their businesses, so they can offer jobs to other local workers, keeping them in the country, too. Not only that, but microfinance provides opportunities for those looking for an alternative path as they heal and avoid what is often a temptation to return to their former trade.

> Christ-centered microfinance in Moldova is a cornerstone for rebuilding in a country riddled with poverty and corruption.

By offering small to medium sized loans, organizations like Invest-Credit in Moldova pave the way for local entrepreneurs to break the cycle of poverty and trafficking in their own lives and in the lives of others in their communities. Christ-centered microfinance in Moldova (and elsewhere) is a cornerstone for rebuilding in a country riddled with poverty and corruption.

No Easy Path

People who have suffered repeated, horrific trauma have no easy path toward rehabilitation. There is no silver bullet. The road to health is long, hard, and may be filled with setbacks and relapses.

Like many who are vulnerable to trafficking, some young women and men have not been given the tools necessary to integrate into society, build self-awareness and confidence, or acquire the knowledge needed to identify and avoid exploitation.[12] As a result, marginalization often leads to further marginalization along family lines. Sometimes, women are exploited by their own husbands and sold to neighbors, or left by their husbands who have found a "better" family. These women have a high mountain to climb to find hope.

And where can they find it?

Organizations like Beginning of Life (BOL) are crucial to breaking the cycle of exploitation. BOL says it is on a mission to see community transformation through holistic development and social justice. This local organization employs only Moldovans and uses a holistic approach to restore and rehabilitate victims of human trafficking in order to plant seeds of dignity in their hearts.

Providing both rehabilitative programming and vocational training equips participants to earn an income. After teaching them trades such as sewing or handcrafting, BOL buys the art or clothing these women create and resells the products in its shop. Ultimately, BOL recognizes and celebrates dignity, worth, opportunity, and hope—the missing pieces in the minds and hearts of countless women who have been robbed by trafficking.

Like all of us, these young women and men need to be reminded of their worth. While no organization can erase trauma, BOL and other like-minded organizations focus on helping these individuals learn to live with their traumatic experiences, to move forward and manage a new life in light of their past. They focus on preparing them for a better future.

Slowly and painfully, the wounded begin to heal. Their breached defenses are repaired, and their souls begin to soften. Serghei Mihailov, executive director of BOL, notes, "Because in the mind of a person who was exploited, first of all, they are deprived of dignity [...] and when they start to produce something, a doll or [something], they get this self esteem or this dignity that 'I created something'... most of their life they were convinced that they were good for nothing [...] They are learning by doing." They develop the strong ethics and discipline needed to build, create, and dream. Vocational training and economic opportunity are crucial to this end.

A Place for Hope

Organizations such as Invest-Credit, Beginning of Life, The Salvation Army, and Open Gate International have a critical role to play in the reshaping of Moldovan society. Entrepreneurship is a key part of rehabilitation and a necessary focal point in the education of Moldovan youth.

New ideas must be encouraged, jobs must be provided, and innovation must be fueled. Equipping individuals with tools, vocational training, education, and loans is imperative to preventing all forms of trafficking.

Equipping might look like a job verification program, such as the one offered by The Salvation Army. This program makes sure that a job in a neighboring country is legitimate and not linked to a brothel.

Equipping might look like a prefabrication factory, in partnership with a group such as Open Gate International. The factory provides jobs to the men of a local village, so they don't have to leave the country, thereby keeping families intact.

Or equipping might look like an after-school culinary program, such as the one run by Open Gate International. This approach equips young girls with the skills necessary to find jobs in the culinary profession.

Equipping could also look like providing a loan for someone who has previously been exploited. Perhaps she has learned how to sew or bake since that time, and a loan could help her to buy a sewing machine or open a bakery.

These efforts, and many like them, will help to change Moldova. Every one of them throws sand into the gearbox of the criminal schemes that prey on the vulnerable.

Hope comes through economic empowerment.

Brave, Jesus-following people live and work in Moldova. These men and women see opportunity, have a vision for change, and have fortified themselves with resilience and stamina to stand their ground and push for transformation. They have the courage to believe in a better future for their country, and their vision and persistence has started to shift the tide for the next generation.

Because of them, there *is* hope. And because God is with them, there is *great* hope.

Kids Win with
Freedom from Trafficking

According to the UN, human trafficking affects every country in the world. While more than 90 percent of countries have legislation criminalizing human trafficking, the number of convictions globally has remained very low.[13] More than 24.9 million victims are trapped in modern-day slavery, with 4.8 million (19 percent) having been sexually exploited.[14]

Trafficking occurs more frequently in less developed countries, where populations are more vulnerable due to factors like poverty.[15] Studies show a concerning increase in the number of detected child trafficking victims, especially girls under the age of eighteen.[16] Globally, children make up a third of all detected trafficking victims, and two of every three child victims are girls.[17]

Kids win with Freedom from Trafficking through Christ-centered microfinance.

This story showed how kids win through
Christ-centered microfinance in these additional areas:

 Valuing Work   Spiritual Growth

Chapter Eleven

Kids Win with
Post-Disaster Rebuilding
A Crucial Stepping Stone

There was little left to take, but the earthquake wanted that too.

Jean Louis Elimés was a single father who had two children. If somebody asked how he earned his living, Elimés might point to his hammer, a palm full of nails, and the cabinet he had just fixed before sundown.

Furniture making, under the umbrella of God's goodness, had for many years secured the income he needed to meet his family's needs. It provided enough food to quiet his children's hungry stomachs, and it kept clean clothes on their bodies. Even though his home felt crowded, his family could sleep soundly and fearlessly there.

That was before the 2010 earthquake dropped Elimés and the entire nation of Haiti into chaos. Thirty-five seconds of terror broke loose in the country, altering its future forever.

Hobbling Through the Rubble

Photographs of the disaster show rubble strewn about, crumpled cars, and broken walls blocking streets. But photographs, by their nature, cherry-pick stones from a mountain of heartache.

The greatest sorrow for Elimés came from watching his children's faces contort with anguish. The earthquake shook his house into a pile of rubble. He couldn't bathe the white dust of destruction from his children's hair and skin. Nowhere he looked could Elimés find drinking water to wet their tongues . . . and he was only one father living in an entire nation of hungry, thirsty survivors.

> The earthquake killed 300,000 residents and left 2.3 million people without food or drinkable water.[1] Some 2,000-4,000 victims had to have limbs amputated after falling rubble crushed their bodies.

The earthquake killed 300,000 residents and left 2.3 million people without food or drinkable water.[1] Some 2,000-4,000 victims had to have limbs amputated after falling rubble crushed their bodies.[2] Children and adults alike hobbled through the ruins, some blinded, most wheezing, others with deep gashes on their faces. The earthquake separated hundreds of sons and daughters from their parents, some temporarily and others for eternity.

Elimés bowed his head to heaven, thanking Almighty God that he could still hug his own kids. The struggle now would be to discover how to provide for his children's most basic needs.

Furniture from Ruins

Thousands of suddenly homeless Haitians clustered on the streets, erecting makeshift homes from tarps, bedsheets, and wooden poles. Entire blocks soon looked like huge canopies of clotheslines and fabric.

Elimés led his family to one of these homeless camps, a decision he'd quickly regret. At night, lying on the ground, he and his children heard shouts and screams as hunger-crazed survivors boldly rummaged through neighboring tents, robbing and assaulting one another.

His son began clutching at Elimés' shirt, begging that they might please sleep somewhere inside. But there was no "inside" where they could go. No one in Haiti seemed to have anything better than what they already had found.

What was Elimés supposed to say to his children? What *could* he say? In those tormenting moments, Elimés would look at his son's wide, silvery eyes and feel his knees tremble. He felt like a failure, incapable of taking care of his children's basic needs: safety, shelter, food, and water.

And then, Elimés had an idea. If he used his furniture-making skills to piece together something saleable, could he earn some cash? And with cash, could he hoist his family

Haiti

Haiti, the poorest country in the Western Hemisphere, has a GDP per capita of $870 (2018) and a Human Development Index ranking of 163 out of 188 countries.[3] Around 2.6 million Haitians live below the international poverty line, on less than $1.90 per day.[4] Haiti faces economic and social challenges exacerbated by its vulnerability to natural disasters, with more than 90 percent of the population at risk.[5]

In 2010, a magnitude 7.0 earthquake struck Haiti, affecting three million people.[6] Many around the world joined to help, and the United Nations estimates that since the earthquake, donors have pledged more than $10 billion of aid to Haiti.[7] Despite all of this aid, sources claim that much of the money has been mismanaged through projects with limited success. In addition, a dangerous culture of aid dependency has emerged as international aid staff perform functions better carried out by local officials.[8] Even a decade after the earthquake, thousands of Haitians still live in displaced people's camps.[9]

out of their poverty? Some might reply, "Wishful thinking." Maybe so. But Elimés could think of no better solution.

For days, Elimés scavenged the stricken landscape, looking for anything that could pass for reusable materials—splintered wood, bent nails, scrap metals. He poked his head beneath clumps of junk and dug through heaps of shattered cinder blocks. With hard work, he discovered wood and other building materials, put up a shop on an open street corner, and set his hands to work.

All the while, the blazing sun slapped its giant thumb against his sweat-glistening forehead. He juggled slabs of wood in his arms as beads of perspiration tumbled from his palms, splashing onto the materials and splotching them with dampness. The sun, brutal and narrow, ground its sharp teeth into his skin. After toiling for hours, Elimés fell to the ground and glared at his supplies, at his hands. What in the world could he do without any actual tools? He could pound nails with stones, sure and easy. But how could he tighten bolts or cut metal without the proper equipment?

So he sat, Elimés, father of two, fortunate to see his family survive the earthquake but fearful he would have to watch them fall prey to malnourishment and dehydration. It could happen. It seemed bound to happen, inevitable, as sure as the sun would burn him again tomorrow.

But some people of God working around the clock in devastated Haiti intervened.

A Holistic Approach to Poverty

A Christian organization called Compassion International gave Elimés a fresh chance to succeed. This Christ-centered, church-based, child-focused organization strives to release children from poverty in Jesus' name.[10]

Following the 2010 earthquake, Compassion took a holistic approach to relieving child poverty in Haiti and launched several microfinance projects. Through this initiative, the group met Elimés and quickly selected him to train in one of its programs. Soon afterward, he got certified to receive a loan.

This opportunity felt to Elimés like a tangible smile from his good Lord. With the loan, he could buy tools; with tools, he could make furniture; and by selling furniture, he could make an income. Elimés immediately bought equipment, rented a small shop, and hired seven employees to work in his new store.

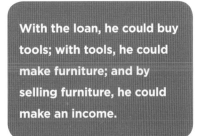

With the loan, he could buy tools; with tools, he could make furniture; and by selling furniture, he could make an income.

He made money slowly but surely, and he repaid his loans in the same way. Because of his on-time payments, he earned classification as a preferred customer.

As the months passed, Elimés became financially capable of regularly providing food for his son and daughter. He gathered the funds to begin building a three bedroom house, a goal his children relished as they dreamed once again of sleeping inside somewhere safe.

To this day, Andre and Mimose marvel at their father, seeing how hard he works to care for them and how much he cherishes them still. Andre, now eighteen, often reflects about how much they once feared sleeping outside and how far the family has come. Even though the earthquake crumbled his former home into dust, Elimés was able to give his children a new home, in large part because of Christ-centered microfinance.

Not only did the loan given to Elimés provide tangible blessing to his family, but with it, he also blessed his community by giving jobs to other men in need. He gets constant orders from customers and now dreams of securing a bigger loan to build a "showroom" where he can display his creations.

Compassion's microfinance program has restored hope to Elimés as a father and as a man able to care for his family. When he thinks of the future, he chuckles. "I believe in myself, that I am a strong man and an able worker," he says. "Should I find a loan again, my children will continue to live much better lives. The future will be secure and I will be able to pay their college tuition."

The earthquake took nearly everything, yes, but because of the kindness of God's people and because of a Christ-centered microfinance loan, it did not take the hope from Elimés' heart. And hope is a wonderful catalyst for healing.

A Blessing to Many

Elimés and his children are only one of many families that Compassion helped after the devastating earthquake. The Cerisieux family in Leogane also saw their lives revolutionized by the microfinance loan program.

The 2010 disaster left Andre Marie Anette—along with her husband, three sons, and niece—without any fence or walls around their home. Fortunately, one of her sons, Emmanuel, participated in Compassion's child sponsorship program, and through this connection, Anette received training to qualify for a loan. After meeting the program's requirements, she accessed her loan and, with another son, Michael, invested in a computer school.

Michael, a skilled student of computer science, had a big dream to establish Internet connections throughout his devastated village. He also wanted to help his mom start a computer literacy school, a brand new venture in their community. To help it succeed, Michael walked from door to door in his village, advertising the school. Eventually, he found three children eager to become his first students—enough to get started. Michael launched the school, and as time passed and as the school's reputation grew, more students came trickling in.

Before long, other local schools reached out to Michael and begged for computer literacy training. Seeing her son succeed made Anette beam like nothing else. Despite the widespread destruction still so evident all around Haiti, good feelings developed within the Cerisieux family circle.

"Our loan gave us success in life, as many people looked to us to train their children," Michael said. "If it hadn't been for that loan, it would have been impossible to cope with our life situation after that disaster."

Because of the loan, Michael believes his family's future is secure. "We have laid the foundation to expand the school's borders to have a 'High Tech School' to train youth in the village," he said. "They will not need to go to the capital city of Port-au-Prince to learn about computers, which would expose them to the danger of traveling back and forth on the highways."

With additional income from the computer school, Michael has been able to build a new house for his soon-to-be wife. "I will be married this coming July to my beloved bride," he said, smiling broadly.

Michael's sibling, Pierre Emanuel, likewise feels very grateful for the loan. "With the loan investment," he said, "my mother was able to pay my tuition, along with the other expenses [incurred] when sending me to college to study diplomacy and political sciences. My dream is to become a diplomat to serve my country abroad."

Since he opened his school of computer literacy, Michael has graduated hundreds of students, each certified and fully knowledgeable in the use of computers. Other schools in Leogane village continue to seek him out to host seminars and classes on computer training.

Since he opened his school of computer literacy, Michael has graduated hundreds of students, each certified and fully knowledgeable in the use of computers.

But none of this—whether the success of the Cerisieux family, or Michael's marriage and new home, or entire communities and villages developing competencies in computer literacy—would have taken place without a microfinance loan.

A Challenge to Get Ahead

In a country where endless amounts of humanitarian aid seems to flow in, often discouraging local entrepreneurship and pushing out many businesses, it can become a challenge to get ahead. But access to loan capital affords individuals the opportunity to grow businesses that can radically change a family's circumstances.

Not only could Elimés and Michael provide for the immediate needs of their own families, they could also build new homes and employ others. By blessing one family with an opportunity to start a business, hundreds of others also have improved their lives.

Despite a life-shattering natural disaster, Haiti stands a little taller today because of the stepping stone provided by Christ-centered microfinance loans.

Kids Win with
Post-Disaster Rebuilding

Every year, natural disasters kill approximately 90,000 individuals and affect about 160 million people globally.[11] Natural disasters have immediate, life-altering impact, often resulting in loss of life, broken infrastructure, and destruction of property. The immediate impact of a natural disaster requires relief efforts through aid to provide basic necessities such as food, shelter, clothing, water, and medical assistance. Disasters also have longer-term consequences that impact economic growth and development, especially affecting the well-being and survival of those who are the most vulnerable and at high risk.[12] While aid is helpful to provide immediate relief, it carries the risk of creating a culture of dependency. More sustainable options are needed to rebuild for the long term. Microfinance programs provide an opportunity for communities to rebuild and become self-sufficient after natural disasters.

Kids win with Post-Disaster Rebuilding through Christ-centered microfinance.

This story showed how kids win through
Christ-centered microfinance in these additional areas:

 Valuing Work

 Improved Housing

 Thriving Families

Sufficient Food

Chapter Twelve

Kids Win: Calculating the Impact

About 7.8 billion people live on our planet.[1] Approximately 1.7 billion are unbanked, with no access to financial tools needed to secure savings, grow businesses, and thereby improve their lives.[2] The World Bank projects that almost 750 million people, about 10 percent of the global population, still lives below the international poverty line (also referred to as "extreme poverty").[3] People in extreme poverty are those who live on less than $1.90 a day (based on 2011 prices and updated to about $2.16 per day in 2019).[4] Half of those in extreme poverty are found in five countries across South Asia and sub-Saharan Africa (India, Nigeria, Democratic Republic of Congo, Ethiopia, and Bangladesh).[5] Of the 750 million living in extreme poverty, only 2.5 percent live in the United States.[6]

Photo: ICM

Residents of the U.S., the richest nation in the world, give more than those in any other country.[7] However, only 6 percent of charitable contributions from the U.S. go to international charities.[8] In addition, although approximately 30 percent of the world population is Christian, only 6 percent of microfinance is Christ-centered, caring for both physical and spiritual needs.[9, 10]

We'd like to take you into the details of three Christ-centered microfinance organizations. We'll show you how to calculate the cost to impact the life of one child for a year … maybe forever. We'll also show you proof that helping parents through Christ-centered microfinance also helps their kids.

International Care Ministries (ICM)

"I'm so thankful to God for all he has done through ICM. I feel God's love, and now I can dream again for my children's future."

Evangeline,

ICM Transform Participant

Photo: ICM

International Care Ministries (ICM) partners with local pastors in the Philippines to help the ultra-poor—those living on less than 50 cents per family member per day. ICM is known and respected for rigorous testing and measuring of its programs. One program, Transform, uses training combined with microfinance to give families hope. Through Transform, participants reported a 106 percent increase in income, 28 percent decrease in illness, and 42 percent increase in self-worth.[11] Results show that the number of children meeting math and phonics proficiency tripled for those whose parents participate in this program.[12]

Evangeline, pictured above, says as she began applying the simple lessons learned each week, she felt amazed by what she could do. She now runs a store from her home, feeds her children three meals a day, and has savings for the first time in her life.

ICM also has a savings group program called Prevail, with a cost per member of $12.34 per year.[1] Given an average family size of 4.7 in the

I $317,000 divided by 25,672 members

Philippines, the cost to impact one child for a year is $2.63.[11] In ICM's 2018/2019 annual report, David Sutherland, Chairman of the Board, states, "The fully loaded cost, across all ICM programs, to help one child for a year is $10."[13] We calculate the actual cost to be $9.31, as follows:

ICM cost to impact one child's life for a year

Total expected costs across all programs in 2018/2019		**$10,019,000**
Total expected people to be served in 2018/2019	*229,000*	
Average household size in the Philippines per UN report	*4.7*	
Total family members that benefit from ICM services	*1,076,300*	**1,076,300**
Cost per person ($10,019,000 divided by 1,076,300)		**$9.31**

VisionFund

As the microfinance arm of World Vision, VisionFund is the largest Christian owner-operator microfinance network in the world. In 2018, the program served 1.1 million clients with a loan portfolio of $727 million.[III] [14] The loans helped to strengthen client businesses and increase incomes. This, in turn, improved the lives of more than 1 million employees and the lives of roughly 4.1 million children, who had more nutritious food, better clothing, and the opportunity to go to school.[IV] [15] VisionFund's programs

Photo: VisionFund

include a focus on serving rural and agriculture-based businesses with microloans, financial services, expert advice, and training.[16]

II $12.34 divided by the average household size in the Philippines of 4.7
III These numbers exclude clients and children in the Cambodia program, which was sold in 2018.
IV These numbers exclude clients and children in the Cambodia program, which was sold in 2018.

Children impacted by VisionFund: 4,100,000

Eastern Europe	93,000
Latin America	518,000
Africa	2,567,000
Asia	922,000

VisionFund focuses on loans rather than savings groups. Loan programs cost more but tend to have greater economic impact. We calculate VisionFund's cost to impact one child's life for a year to be $12.72.

VisionFund cost to change one child's life for a year

Total cost of program		**$85,535,000**
Number of children served in 2018 (including Cambodia for part of the year)	4,577,000	
Total number of microfinance clients	1,228,000	
Assumed people benefiting through the program (other parent or dependents)	921,000	
Total people benefiting through the program	6,726,000	**6,726,000**
Cost per person ($85,535,000 divided by 6,726,000)		**$12.72**

Furthermore, the charitable contribution required to impact one child's life for a year is only $1.55. This is because VisionFund's large loan portfolio generates significant interest income which offsets costs.

HOPE International

HOPE International invests in the dreams of families in the world's underserved communities as it proclaims and lives the gospel. The organization shares the hope of Christ as it provides biblically based training, savings services, and loans designed to restore dignity and break the cycle of poverty. HOPE serves more than one million families across sixteen countries, thereby impacting the lives of millions of children. In a recent report, the organization states:

"We believe one of the best ways to care for children living in poverty is to empower their parents. Parents in the HOPE network receive training, build savings accounts, and start businesses to provide for their children's needs rather than rely on outside charities or services."[17]

HOPE lays out the concept and the process in its 2018 annual report:

We empower parents to provide for their families and communities.

MEETING BASIC NEEDS

As families expand small businesses or accumulate savings, they can make their home more comfortable and are better prepared for emergency expenses. Financial stability means parents can provide more consistently for their family's basic needs.

PRIORITIZING EDUCATION

When families struggle to put food on the table, household budget adjustments often cut out long-term investments like education. But as household income and savings increase, children go to school more consistently.

DISCIPLING CHILDREN

As HOPE-network clients receive discipleship and training, they understand God's love more deeply. In closer communion with God, parents are better equipped to disciple their children, leading them to the truth of God's Word.

COMMUNITIES TRANSFORM

With greater financial stability, parents have more margin to meet needs around them—paying for food or medical costs for struggling neighbors, starting small schools or kids' programs, supporting their churches, and even adopting children.

GENERATIONS CHANGE

As parents model wise financial habits for their children and invest in them physically, emotionally, and spiritually, they prepare their children for greater independence and maturity as adults. These choices weaken the generational grip of poverty.

Icons and Text: HOPE International

My children see me as a successful and hard worker. Sometimes they tell me that they think we are the richest people here in our community."

Photo: HOPE International

The cost to serve one client for a year across all of HOPE's programs is $19.37.[18] The UN average household size averaged across the sixteen countries where HOPE operates is 4.01.[19, 20] $19.37 divided by 4.01 is $4.83. The detailed calculation is as follows.

HOPE International's cost to impact one child's life for a year

Cost to serve one client for a year[21]					**$19.37**
Average household size per UN	2	3	4	5	
Rwanda					4.3
Ukraine					2.5
Dominican Republic					3.5
Republic of Congo					4.3
Philippines					4.7
Moldova					2.8
Romania					2.7
Burundi					4.8
Zambia					5.1
Malawi					4.5
Zimbabwe					4.1
Peru					3.8
Paraguay					4.6
Undisclosed Country #1					3.4
Undisclosed Country #2					4.6
Haiti					4.4
Subtotal					64.1
Divided by the number of countries					16
Average household size of these countries					4.01 **4.01**
Cost per person ($19.37 divided by 4.01)					**$4.83**

The Numbers Line Up

This graph summarizes each organization's approximate cost to impact one child's life for a year:

ICM

Across all programs — $9.31

Savings groups only — $2.63

VisionFund

Across all programs — $12.72

Across all programs (less interest income) — $1.55

HOPE International

Across all programs — $4.83

An Alternative Calculation

We can also calculate the incredible impact per dollar of microfinance in a completely different way. We based the calculation above on the cost to help one child for a year. In microlending, loans are repaid and can be used repeatedly. The interest on the loans can cover program costs, such that any additional contributions can be used to expand the loan portfolio. In addition, as clients pay off their loans, more and more people can be helped. VisionFund has a calculator on its website (visionfund.org/donation-impact). Here, you can see the number of children impacted initially and how that number grows over time. A $1,000 contribution, for example, initially helps twenty nine children, but after five years, that number grows to 151 children. Accordingly, a contribution of $1,000, divided by 151 children helped, is $6.62 to impact one child.

No matter how you calculate it, the impact per giving dollar through Christ-centered microfinance is profound.

Does it really help the kids?

To prove that $4.83 really impacts the life of a child, we leaned on our friend Rich Fox, a CFO and professor in data analytics. After receiving raw data from several organizations, Rich reviewed and analyzed the information and confirmed the organizations' claims that when Christ-centered microfinance organizations come alongside parents, the kids win.

> Such data confirms our intuition. As it relates to at least one child well-being outcome, somewhere between 96-99 percent of the time, Parent(s) + Opportunity = Kids Win.

VisionFund, it turns out, has a treasure trove of data regarding the effect of microfinance on the kids of clients. Overlapping several of our Kids Win areas, the organization has identified eight "child well-being outcomes": sufficient food, basic education, additional clothing and shoes, affordable healthcare, sufficient drinking water, improved sanitation, improved housing, and youth learning opportunities.

VisionFund's 2017 survey included responses from 119,111 clients living in seven countries: Cambodia, Dominican Republic, Honduras, Mexico, Mongolia, Myanmar, and the Philippines.[21] The raw data Rich analyzed confirms that:

- 96 percent of those surveyed reported improvement in at least one child well-being outcome.[22]
- 74 percent of those surveyed reported improvement in at least two child well-being outcomes.[23]
- 57 percent of those surveyed reported improvement in three or more child well-being outcomes.[24]

The following year, VisionFund surveyed 89,072 clients in Myanmar alone.[25] This survey revealed even better child well-being outcomes than those reported in 2017.[26] In 2018, 99 percent of those surveyed reported improvement in at least one child well-being outcome, while 69 percent of clients reported improvements in three or more of the outcomes.[27]

In both sets of data, the top improvements in child well-being outcomes were (in order) sufficient food, improved basic education, and additional clothing/shoes.[28, 29]

Such data confirms our intuition. As it relates to at least one child well-being outcome, somewhere between 96-99 percent of the time, Parent(s) + Opportunity = Kids Win.

Other Considerations

In the classic business book, *Good to Great*, Jim Collins studied companies over a forty-year period to see whether he could identify common characteristics of companies that became great.[30] He could. One of the concepts he talked about, the "flywheel" effect, is summarized by Expert Program Management's website.[31]

Imagine a very large flywheel. Thousands of kilograms or pounds in weight. To get it to spin you need to start pushing it. As you first start to push, it seems almost impossible to turn. But you keep at it. Pushing it, and pushing it, and pushing it. The more momentum you build up, the easier it gets; but you still need to keep pushing hard.

Then at some point.... this giant flywheel takes on a life of its own and it's spinning really fast and doesn't need as much effort to spin.

In fact, now it's really difficult to stop! We have achieved a Good to Great Flywheel Effect. We are taking consistent action.... We are achieving visible results. This, in turn, energizes people and momentum is easy to sustain without much effort.

The flywheel effect works in business and in life. Christ-centered microfinance generates long-term, cumulative, benefits. It works over time, sometimes over a lifetime. Sometimes over generations.

This concept proves out in our review of the raw data. Rich confirmed that, as a parent receives a loan, pays it back, and then gets another loan,

> Christ-centered microfinance generates long-term, cumulative, benefits. It works over time, sometimes over a lifetime. Sometimes over generations.

the benefits to the child continue to increase. So yes, Christ-centered microfinance does work; it works over time, and its impact on parents and children alike can be enormous.

In *Shrewd Samaritan*, Bruce Wydick talks about the importance of Christians learning to love with their hearts and their heads.[32] We agree! He created a methodology of evaluating charities based on the combination of effectiveness, cost, and the importance to human flourishing.[33] Based on these criteria, he gives microfinance a four out of five star rating.[34] Four stars out of five is pretty good. However, upon review, we can see that Bruce focused his analysis on microfinance, not on *Christ-centered* microfinance:

1. He refers exclusively to studies focused on secular microfinance. None of the seven studies referenced Christ-centered microfinance.

2. The studies Wydick referenced all involved saturated markets. Christ-centered microfinance generally focuses on places not so saturated and, in many cases, which have no banking services at all. (In fact, in 2018, VisionFund sold its operations in Cambodia, stating that this market had matured and that the organization intended to redeploy assets in markets where greater need existed.)[35]

Later in the book, Wydick strikingly acknowledges, "there is an increasing body of evidence that spiritually based, holistic interventions yield long-term impacts, not just on spiritual beliefs but on 'secular' economic outcomes. While there is more research that can be done to better understand the mechanisms behind holistic, integrated development, it is exciting to see mounting evidence of its fruit."[36] So, when considering Christ-centered microfinance, we are confident the rating should be five out of five stars!

Some Final Thoughts

Please understand what we're *not* saying. We're not saying that we should stop pulling children out of human trafficking. That noble task absolutely needs to continue. We're also not saying child sponsorship is wrong. We sponsor several kids through such programs and know them to be effective.

What we *are* saying is that Christ-centered microfinance helps keep families together and enables parents to provide for their children the way God intended.

Based on intuition and data, Christ-centered microfinance is simply the most efficient and effective way to help kids. If the goal is to impact the greatest number of children possible, then at $4.83 to impact the life of one child for a year microfinance beats everything else—hands down.

Kids Win:
Calculating the Impact

This chapter showed how kids win through Christ-centered microfinance in all 10 kids win areas.

Valuing Work

Adequate Healthcare

Thriving Families

Sufficient Food

Sufficient Clothing

Basic Education

Spiritual Growth

Freedom from Trafficking

Improved Housing

Post-Disaster Rebuilding

Kids win: Calculating the Impact through Christ-centered microfinance.

Chapter Thirteen

How You Win, Too

In most cases, the best place for a kid to be is with his or her parents. That's because, in general, parents love and protect their kids like no one else.

Christ-centered microfinance can help parents pull themselves out of material, spiritual, emotional, and relational poverty. When this happens, everyone wins, both parents and their kids.

And they aren't the only ones who win.

You Win Too

We hope that in reading this book, you'll enter into, continue, and deepen your involvement with Christ-centered microfinance. We believe your involvement will help you to:

- ♦ Celebrate the innate value of work
- ♦ Grow in thankfulness
- ♦ Experience the benefits of generosity
- ♦ Gain eternal perspective and rewards

Celebrate the Innate Value of Work

Ephesians 2:10 declares, "We are His workmanship created in Christ Jesus for good works that He prepared in advance that we may walk in them."[1] What a joy to know God has prepared things in advance for us to do and accomplish! Work is a gift from God and has implications for the joy, purpose, dignity, and meaning we derive in life. It is not a chore or an obligation; it is a provision.

Christ-centered microfinance plays a significant role in providing recipients with the opportunity to work, often in situations where little opportunity to work existed before. This is a gift for our brothers and sisters in developing countries where jobs might be scarce and opportunity slim. The children highlighted throughout this book have learned the value of hard work and discipline through watching their parents. In the same way, your children learn by watching you.

Involvement with Christ-centered microfinance provides an opportunity for us and our families to see and talk about the value and blessing of work. Consider the ways you can instill this value and sense of calling in your own children.

> Christ-centered microfinance provides an opportunity for us and our families to see and talk about the value and blessing of work.

Perhaps you can set your kids up with a bake sale, or help them to wash cars, or teach them to collect and recycle bottles and cans, so they can learn about the process of earning money through their own efforts.

Or you might consider taking it a step further and give them a small loan to buy what they need to run a lemonade stand. After they've done the work and paid back the loan, you can teach them about stewardship, inviting them to keep part of the earnings and give the rest away, perhaps to a Christ-centered microfinance organization. Whatever you do, help them to experience the satisfaction and blessing of working, earning money, and celebrating the results.

We believe so deeply in impressing these values upon children that we've developed a list of ideas to help you and your family (see Appendix B). There are so many creative ways we can help kids value work. Valuing work will help shape their worldview and impact their understanding of poverty. The bottom line is this: your involvement with Christ-centered microfinance will help you and your family to understand, appreciate, and experience the blessing of walking in the good works God prepared beforehand for YOU!

Grow in Thankfulness

The Apostle Paul tells us in 1 Thessalonians 5:16-18 to "rejoice always, pray continually, give thanks in all circumstances; for this is God's will for you in Christ Jesus."[2] In a similar way, the psalmist proclaims in Psalm 107:1, "Oh give thanks to the Lord, for He is good, for His lovingkindness is everlasting."[3] God made us with the capacity to give thanks, but we must choose to express our thanks.

> Consider this charge: recognize your material blessings, realize the opportunities you have, and let these things spark thankfulness in your heart.

So many people around the world have so little. As mentioned earlier, 1.7 billion people remain unbanked, while 750 million people live on less than $1.90 per day.[4,5] Our brothers and sisters benefiting from the powerful work of Christ-centered microfinance often see dramatic changes in their circumstances, which may reawaken them to God's provision and to hearts of thankfulness.

Many of us in wealthier nations face a different set of challenges. We are surrounded by images in TV shows, movies, articles, and social media that encourage us to compare ourselves to superficial, romanticized, idealistic images of "perfection." This system makes it tempting to lean into these things and entertain the thought, *but if I just had…*

The New York Times ran an article about millionaires who don't feel rich. It stated, "many such accomplished and ambitious members of the digital elite still do not think of themselves as particularly fortunate, in part because they are surrounded by people with more wealth—often a lot more."[6] It is human nature to compare ourselves with those who have more, but the reality is that virtually the entire world has less than us.

The point is not to compare ourselves to the person who has little and think "we're better" or "we're more blessed," but to accept that we are blessed. We can choose thankfulness.

If you're reading this book, it's likely you have everything you need and most of what you want. The Global Rich List reports that if you make $30,000 per year (after taxes), you will be in the top 1.23% of earners in the world.[7] You're likely one of the wealthiest people on the planet!

Your involvement with Christ-centered microfinance will help you to steady the unstable parts of your soul that struggle with finding thankfulness. Consider this charge: recognize your material blessings, realize the opportunities you have, and let these things spark thankfulness in your heart.

Experience the Benefits of Generosity

> You don't have to be rich, and you don't have to give much, to reap the rewards of generosity.

Studies have shown that generous people are happier people and more likely to be increasingly generous.[8] The Bible overflows with verses about giving and generosity. How amazing is it that we get to be blessed as a result of our generosity? 2 Corinthians 9:6 says, "Now this I say, he who sows sparingly shall also reap sparingly; and he who sows bountifully shall also reap bountifully. Let each one do just as he has purposed in heart; not under compulsion; for God loves a cheerful giver."[9]

You don't have to be rich, and you don't have to give much, to reap the rewards of generosity.[10, 11] In fact, a common practice in lending and savings groups is the establishment of a community fund. Many groups will set aside funds each time they meet in order to help those in their community when they have need. They build in the opportunity to be generous.

Even more so than our brothers and sisters around the world, we have the means to be generous, even if it's just a little. We don't give because we're saviors. We give because God invites us to give, because we have more than enough, and because there's blessing in giving.

> We don't give because we're saviors. We give because God invites us to give, because we have more than enough, and because there's blessing in giving.

Your involvement in Christ-centered microfinance gives you an opportunity to practice generosity and to model it to your kids. We all have to start somewhere. If we have $10 and don't feel comfortable giving away $1, what happens if we have more? Perhaps, then, if we have $10,000, we won't feel comfortable giving away $1,000. Generosity is learned. How about starting with as little as $4.83?

Maybe this looks like giving up a trip to the coffee shop once a week or once a month and stashing the extra $4.83 to help one child for a year through the power of Christ-centered microfinance. Or maybe you can consider giving $4.83 a month to one of the great causes profiled in this book (see Appendix C). Imagine the legacy of generosity you can leave through the small (or large!), consistent actions you take to be generous.

God instilled in each of us the ability to be a cheerful giver. Christ-centered microfinance is an excellent outlet for generosity that will encourage you toward a life of increased joy and bounty as you invest in the lives of others.

Gain Eternal Perspective and Rewards

The Bible is clear that we get to heaven through our faith in Jesus Christ, not by our works.[12,13] However, our good works still matter and result in eternal rewards. This is confirmed by the apostle Paul as he writes:

Consider investing in the lives of children through Christ-centered microfinance. The Bible promises eternal rewards for your faithfulness.

"For no one can lay any foundation other than the one already laid, which is Jesus Christ. If anyone builds on this foundation using gold, silver, costly stones, wood, hay or straw, their work will be shown for what it is, because the Day will bring it to light. It will be revealed with fire, and the fire will test the quality of each person's work. If what has been built survives, the builder will receive a reward."[14] God will reward us in heaven for our earthly involvement in His purposes.

Matthew 6:19-20 states, "do not store up for yourselves treasures on earth where moths and rust destroy, and thieves break in and steal, but store up for yourself treasures in heaven where neither moths nor rust destroys, and thieves do not break in and steal."[15] How do we store up treasures in heaven? We do this by sharing the Gospel and by doing good works. Christ-centered microfinance does both at the same time.

Consider investing in the lives of children through Christ-centered microfinance. The Bible promises eternal rewards for your faithfulness.

A Pound of Gold

We can't buy our way into heaven, of course, and making poor financial investments on this earth won't jeopardize our salvation. But, our Lord Jesus calls His people to conduct themselves with wisdom, which we should use in managing our money. Our Lord has a keen interest in how we use the funds He gives us in this life. We may not feel "rich," but even we can invest our few dollars so wisely, so intentionally,

We may not feel "rich," but even we can invest our few dollars so wisely, so intentionally, that over time they carry immense weight and impact—perhaps, even more than gold.

that over time they carry immense weight and impact—perhaps, even more than gold.

God's amazing plan is unfolding around us. He promises that our involvement will result in growth and blessing. Will we hear His voice and courageously jump in? YES! We may not have much, but we do have $4.83. We will give up that cup of coffee. We will walk a bit farther to avoid paying for big city, downtown parking. We will make the $4.83 investment into the lives and eternities of families around the world. Collectively, we will be part of impacting the lives of millions of children!

Photo: HOPE International

Our $4.83 will not be like a pound of feathers. It will be like a pound of gold!

Jenn's Path to
Christ-centered Microfinance

I have always felt drawn to missions and ministry work. The annual junior high and high school missions trip of my Southern California church often meant a quick but memorable drive to Mexico. We would pack out the church vans and our caravan would trek across the border to a remote orphanage, where we'd pour concrete, paint walls, and drop off shoe boxes full of toiletries for the kids. All of us felt great joy whenever we saw the excitement of the orphans as we pulled up for a visit.

After a few days of hard work in the blazing sun—mixing cement, pouring a sidewalk, painting a dormitory wall, eating authentic Mexican food for each meal—we'd pack up and head home. And then the children and staff would begin an eager countdown until we returned the following year.

By the time we came back twelve months later, however, little had changed. The donated toiletries had vanished, the new soccer balls had deflated, the concrete sidewalk remained half-finished, while the rest of the walls still lacked paint. I didn't think much about it at the time, because this was just "what you do" as a good Christian. We had come to help and to serve, and it felt good to do what we could.

As we drove home, we could pat ourselves on the back for a job well done. We happily celebrated our noble service in sacrificing a full weekend of our normal lives to help the less fortunate. That ugly purple wall? Now a pretty blue! We'd improved the kids' smiles with fresh toothpaste, new toothbrushes, and a few toys. They could even walk on a (partial) sidewalk! We served with pure intentions and honest efforts, eagerly desiring to support a hurting community of children. We thought this was the best way to do it.

> Something deep inside of me, however, couldn't fully accept that our work represented the epitome of service and charity. I felt dissatisfied, but I didn't quite know why.

Something deep inside of me, however, couldn't fully accept that our work represented the epitome of service and charity. I felt dissatisfied, but I didn't quite know why.

A Shift in Perspective

A trip to Uganda during my college years began to shift my perspective. A random selection of individuals from around the United States, all committed to living with and serving a community of people who lived approximately four hours outside of Kampala, the capital, came to Africa to build houses for three families.

Each of the three families had gone through an application process to be selected to receive a "home on loan." The house wouldn't become theirs until they had paid back the cost of the home, about $3,000. They could repay the money in several ways: cash, of course, but also through providing food for laborers working on the home, or by supplying sweat equity to help build their home or the homes of others.

Observing such a model in action changed everything for me. Who worked hardest on the construction sites? The homeowners.

Each day, the wives fixed amazing meals for our team and other laborers. These homes were built by a hard-working community through collaborative effort. I had never experienced *anything* like it. Throughout the process, these families displayed a keen sense of ownership.

Our bonds with the men and women in the community grew stronger with each passing day. Anticipation grew as we laid brick upon brick. We could all feel the energy building every day on the job. This work had *meaning*. Such collaborative work made a lasting difference—and it didn't require us to return the following year.

My heart felt full as we gathered at each site toward the end of our stay to celebrate the completion of the homes. As if the bright, cheek-to-cheek smiles on everyone's faces didn't say enough, the glimmering, laughing eyes spoke, too. Every person there had a tremendous sense of accomplishment and pride. We outsiders had come alongside dedicated men and women and watched as they discovered the deep dignity found in doing hard work, in having ownership of something, in creating.

> We outsiders had come alongside dedicated men and women and watched as they discovered the deep dignity found in doing hard work, in having ownership of something, in creating.

Its beauty nearly overwhelmed me.

The experience also sparked something new in me, a spark that would soon turn into a fire. On that trip, I discovered microfinance and witnessed firsthand how economic development work can transform lives.

Conflicted and Unsure

A few years later, I found myself in a transitional season. I'd moved on from my first job in executive recruiting and felt conflicted and unsure of what might come next. My heart felt split. I loved business and clearly had a gift for it, and yet I also felt passionate about international missions and ministry work.

People all around me suggested I become a pastor and consider ministry full-time. My ill-informed paradigm at the time told me that "to be in ministry is to work for a church or a nonprofit, neither of which operate very effectively. Moreover, if I go into full-time ministry, I'll probably have to sell all I have and move to Africa." I now laugh at the thought, as I've learned a lot since then. But back then, my deep, internal conflict caused me a lot of sleepless nights.

And so began my mission to discover how business and ministry could converge in my life.

Seeking a Deeper Understanding

As a lover of and follower of Jesus, I spent a lot of time over the next year trying to come to a deeper understanding of who I am, why I'm here, and what my next assignment might be. I spent many hours in prayer and had countless conversations with mentors, family, and friends, trying to grasp what others perceived as my strengths. I took on a variety of assignments and even applied to seminary.

Each door I walked through served a purpose and energized a different part of me. As I neared the close of this "seeking season," I settled on going to seminary. I would pursue a Master of Divinity and see how my journey would unfold from there.

One morning, though, I woke up with a nudge from the Holy Spirit. "Jenn," He said to me in an inner-audible kind of way, "you've forgotten that I've also called you to business." I briefly feared I might have to start the journey all over again, but the feeling passed as I recalled the kind of job I wanted to pursue.

It had become crystal clear to me, so plain that the objective portion of my resumé read something like this: "Serve in fundraising, development, or relationship management for a nonprofit or Christian ministry focused on 'business as mission' and located in Orange County." Did something like this even exist? I didn't know. But I sent my resumé to friends and contacts, hoping that *something* might rise to the surface.

As I drove to a job interview one afternoon, my phone buzzed. I quickly glanced at the new email, and the title intrigued me enough that I pulled into a gas station to give it a thorough read. The contents dumbfounded me; I had to reread the email several times.

It came from a guy I'd met nearly a year before. He represented an organization that focused on alleviating both spiritual and physical poverty through Christ-centered microfinance: HOPE International. The group needed someone to manage its fundraising efforts along the West Coast and preferred someone living in Orange County.

> To share the great news of Jesus while equipping underserved men and women with the resources and opportunity to grow a business and pull themselves out of poverty—what could be better?

I responded immediately: "How about me?"

Chris and I connected the next day. Not long afterwards, the organization offered me the job. Thus began one of the greatest adventures of my life.

A Divine Calling

Clearly, God called me into the world of microfinance, at first through my professional efforts and then through my avocational efforts. I love the empowering, dignifying, transformative, life-changing work of these organizations! To share the great news of Jesus while equipping underserved men and women with the resources and opportunity to grow a business and pull themselves out of poverty—what could be better?

My husband, Kevin, and I are fully behind this cause and these efforts, and I hope to see Christ-centered microfinance powerfully impact the lives of millions of others around the globe. I pray that this book, in some small way, can help to make that happen.

Lance's Path to
Christ-centered Microfinance

started my career as a CPA at Arthur Andersen, one of the big international accounting firms. My written life plan included making a gajillion dollars and being out of business and in full-time ministry by age fifty. Life was good.

But in 2002, in a swirl of document-shredding sparked by the Enron scandal in Houston, the firm I had loved and been a part of for twenty years collapsed. Arthur Andersen was supposed to last forever! How could it just be *gone*?

The implosion rocked my world. Weren't good people supposed to be blessed? Why do bad things happen to good people? I had a wife, three kids, a house nearly paid off, and some money in the bank. Was God telling me that I should exit business and go into full-time ministry?

In the middle of this mess, we needed to figure out God's path forward. Jeanie (my wife) and several close friends became an informal advisory board for me. We all started praying.

I had to do a bit of juggling. As I tried to take care of my clients, I began running around for interviews with not-for-profit groups as well as the other big CPA firms. While we prayed, God's plan began to take shape. In the end, we sensed two distinct messages from God:

1. "I made you for business. Stay in business."

2. "Use your business mind to find the highest and best use of *My* money" (that is, stop giving merely to the last person who asked).

So, in May 2002, I landed at PwC (PricewaterhouseCoopers LLP), one of the remaining "Big 4" assurance, tax, and consulting firms. The second message energized me to find organizations that wielded extreme Kingdom impact by their effective use of each giving dollar they received.

> "Use your business mind to find the highest and best use of My money."

What Does God See as Important?

My accountant's mind directed me to create a spreadsheet that evaluated and weighted the factors that I supposed God would consider most important. These factors included such things as:

- ◆ Is this organization meeting both physical and spiritual needs?
- ◆ Is it "teaching people how to fish" or "giving them a fish?"
- ◆ Is it a hand up or a handout?
- ◆ Is it a well-run, efficient organization?
- ◆ If international, does it invite local people to get the job done?
- ◆ Is there high impact per giving dollar?

I began to evaluate charities by running them through my spreadsheet. Over the next few years, I began to zero in on microfinance as the most effective way to use giving dollars. With microfinance, just a little bit of outside help empowers men and women to band together and *pull themselves out of poverty*. Microfinance is extraordinarily efficient. I would say that in the world of charity, it's nothing less than earth-shattering.

Why *Christ-centered* Microfinance?

So I, the business guy, got excited about the power of microfinance. But then Jeanie said something like, "If we really believe in heaven and hell, is it okay to only help someone get a business and be a little more comfortable for the next ten or fifty years? Shouldn't we also focus on their eternity?"

Her comments refocused me on the path of Christian microfinance. The question then became for me, how could I find a superior Christ-centered microfinance organization? Back in 2008, the answer found me.

One day, while I stood out in the courtyard of our church harassing people to join me and my family in an annual Mexico house-building trip, a guy named Mike Lennon came up to me. "I'll come to Mexico and build a house with you," said Mike, "if you'll come to lunch with me and hear about a Christian microfinance organization called HOPE International."

Do you ever get the feeling that God has His fingers on the details of your life?

By the end of my lunch with Mike, I felt pretty sure that our conversation would change my life. I now believe that giving through Christ-centered microfinance has the highest impact per giving dollar of any charity. As a result, I've developed my Top Ten Questions in deciding which charity to support (see our website www.kids-win.com).

"I Want Your Heart"

I quickly got involved in HOPE's local efforts by joining the Southern California regional board. One day, in regards to HOPE, I sensed God saying to me, "Lance, I want your heart."

I didn't get it. Accountants really don't have hearts, do they? Besides, if we did, wouldn't they be connected to our money? And I was already giving my money to HOPE.

"Uhh, God, I'm giving money to HOPE," I prayed, "so you have my heart."

"No, I want your *whole* heart."

"Well, Ok. But what does that mean?"

"It means that I want you to love those people, those clients of HOPE who, on this side of heaven, you will never see. I want you to love them the way I love them."

"Umm, the way *You* love them?"

"Yes, the way I love them."

I'm not always so smart, but immediately I recognized the huge implications of committing to God that I would love *anyone* the way He loves them. There would be life implications, time implications, money implications. Such a commitment would change my life . . . and I *liked* my life.

"No, God. I can't love these people the way you love them. Besides, you're God and I'm not. So, You love them and I'll just give money."

"No, Lance, I want your heart."

"No, I really can't."

"Yes, you can. I want your heart."

> "Ok, God. I give you my heart. My whole heart. I will love those people who, on this side of heaven, I will never see. I will love them the way that you love them. I'm in. I'm all in."

My mental conversation with God seemed to be going in circles. Perhaps you've been there too. You *know* what God wants you to do, but you just don't want to do it. You can run, of course, but God runs right with you. Through His Holy Spirit, He just works you over s-l-o-w-l-y.

I knew what I needed to do to get peace. I had to say "yes."

As I prayed, I began to see that, although it felt risky, it was better to love with both my money *and* my heart. Finally, I gave up control and jumped in.

"Ok, God. I give you my heart. My whole heart. I will love those people who, on this side of heaven, I will never see. I will love them the way that you love them. I will love them through my money and with my whole heart. I'm in. I'm all in."

What About the Kids?

As I continued to grow in my love and commitment to individuals I didn't even know, God started bringing a new thought to my mind.

Both the Christian and secular giving worlds seem to focus a lot on kids. I like that. Kids are more vulnerable and not nearly as capable of providing for their own physical needs as adults. Spiritually, kids tend to be more open; they may not yet have formed a clear worldview. For those reasons, it feels right to focus giving dollars on impacting kids.

My problem was that I had never put Christ-centered microfinance in the "helps kids" bucket. Had I clearly thought through the issue?

Early one morning while driving to work, I prayed. As I listened, I seemed to hear God speaking. He had a clear message for me: "HOPE is for the kids. HOPE is for the kids."

Umm, okay . . . but what did *that* mean: "HOPE is for the kids"?

Only a very small percentage of HOPE's clients are children. By contrast, a large percentage are moms and/or dads with kids. Microfinance is more flexible than traditional jobs and allows parents who have childcare responsibilities to fully participate.

It seemed intuitive to me that if Christ-centered microfinance can help parents pull themselves out of spiritual, emotional, and physical poverty, then their kids will benefit, too. Furthermore, it seemed to me that if a donor cared *only* about helping kids, microfinance to their parents is still the most powerful and most cost-efficient approach. If you help the parents, of course their kids benefit.

But does this "obvious" conclusion prove out in real life? That's what pushed me into doing the research and ultimately co-writing this book with Jenn. The answer is a resounding YES! When parents get opportunities, kids win.

Christ-centered microfinance keeps families together and enables the parent to be the provider. This is God's model. And, there's no additional programming costs required to help the kids—the parents and the community assume the responsibility. At a cost of $4.83 to impact the life of a child for a year, maybe forever, I believe that Christ-centered microfinance is the most effective and efficient way to help kids-period.

"I believe that Christ-centered microfinance is the most effective and efficient way to help kids-period"

Appendix A:
"Kids Win" Website

Go to our website, at www.kids-win.com, to find additional resources, upcoming Christ-centered microfinance events, and videos. We provide helpful materials, such as "ten questions to ask when looking for a Christ-centered microfinance organization to support" and family activities to help you and your children engage more intentionally around the concepts presented in the book.

www.kids-win.com

Valuing Work

Thriving Families

Sufficient Clothing

Spiritual Growth

Improved Housing

Adequate Healthcare

Sufficient Food

Basic Education

Freedom from Trafficking

Post-disaster Rebuilding

Appendix B:
How You Can Make a Difference

Equip, Educate, and Engage your kids

- Have an intentional family discussion with your kids about the following topics:
  - Why work is good and a blessing
  - Understanding our blessings (Go to www.globalrichlist.com to see where you sit in comparison to the world.)
  - The power of $4.83 to change another kid's life
  - Why giving is a blessing and how it improves our lives
- Demonstrate the power of entrepreneurship and how a small investment can create a big impact. Consider giving your kids a small loan, so they can get creative and start a business venture. The important thing is to help kids understand the concept of a loan that they need to pay back. To make it more fun, consider teaching them the basics of interest and the importance of pricing products in such a way as to generate a profit. You can also help them put together a simple budget, so they understand expenses. Here are 10 ideas for simple businesses that are easy for kids to run:
  - Set up a lemonade stand
  - Host a bake sale
  - Propagate succulents and sell them
  - Create glitter pinecones to sell during fall or winter
  - Make dog treats to sell
  - Make bath salts to sell

- Mow lawns for neighbors
- Walk dogs for neighbors
- Feed pets for neighbors
- Wash cars for family or neighbors
- Collect cans or bottles for recycling

Learn

- Visit our website (www.kids-win.com).
- Review our list of organizations and visit their websites to learn more about what they are doing (*see Appendix C*).
- Visit Kiva (www.Kiva.org) and provide a microfinance loan directly to a group or family; the website provides pictures and details about the group or family's story; your loan will be repaid and you can reinvest the money.
- Meet with a representative of an organization we've mentioned and ask questions.
- Attend an annual event or summit hosted by an organization to meet their staff and learn more about their operations.
- Attend a poverty simulation. The HOPE Poverty Simulation is a 2.5-hour immersive learning experience designed to help participants get a glimpse into the realities of a life in extreme poverty. Over the course of the simulation, participants are confronted with a series of challenges that mimic the complex, everyday obstacles that billions of men and women are forced to grapple with in our broken world. The simulation helps build empathy for families living in extreme poverty and prompts strategic thinking about effective responses. Find a Poverty Simulation near you on HOPE's website (https://www.hopeinternational.org/take-action/povertysimulation).
- Check out charity rating sites like Charity Navigator, Excellence in Giving, and Guidestar to learn more about how organizations operate.

Pray

- Pray for your heart to be open to see what God is saying to you about your involvement with Christ-centered microfinance.
- Select a photo from a website we've referenced and pray for that child and his or her family; specifically pray that the child will be blessed in the ten "Kids Win" areas outlined in the preceding chapters.
- Pray for the organizations referenced in this book: for their staff and for those they serve.

Give

- Consider making a donation to one (or several) of the causes in this book. Any amount helps—maybe start with $4.83?
- Even better, how about giving $4.83 a month? Organizations highly value regular, recurring giving as it's very important for their annual planning. Monthly giving, set up in advance, has very little cost to the organization but allows them to count on a regular amount.

Ask How You Can Help

- Many organizations have local/regional people that will know of local awareness and fundraising events you can attend. You could also invite your family and friends to attend with you.
- Consider volunteering at an annual fundraising event:
  - Collect silent auction items
  - Help with setup and registration
- Volunteer to write thank you notes to donors.
- Volunteer to be on the organization's local or regional advisory board.

Go See the Work

- Many organizations organize short-term trips that give participants the opportunity to see the work in the field, meet staff, and visit clients or associates. Depending on the organization and the location of the trip, these can be great opportunities for an entire family.

Get Others Involved

- Once you're engaged, begin to spread the news. Give someone this book!
- Write a review for this book on Amazon and share our book on social media.
- Choose an activity that you can invite others to give toward that will benefit an organization. Consider a 5k/10k walk, a marathon, or a bike ride.
- Invite friends and colleagues to an annual fundraiser.
- Host an event at your home with a guest speaker from an organization and invite your small group, friends, or neighbors.
- Recruit a group of friends to join you on a trip to visit the field or to attend an annual summit.

Appendix C:
Suggested Organizations

We partnered with some amazing organizations to obtain the stories and data found in this book. We encourage you to learn more about these organizations and become a part of helping kids and keeping families together by investing in the dreams of underserved communities.

CHRIST-CENTERED MICROFINANCE ORGANIZATIONS

Center for Community Transformation Group of Ministries (CCT)

Since 1991, CCT has been committed to creating lasting, holistic change among the poor in the Philippines through microfinance loans, entrepreneurial training, mentoring, Bible studies, counseling, and development programs and services. The CCT Group is composed of 16 ministries that reach out to street families, children, youth, micro-entrepreneurs, farmers, fisherfolk, factory workers, informal workers, tribespeople, overseas Filipino workers, and the communities at large.

http://www.cct.org.ph/

Compassion International 501(c)(3)

Since 1952, Compassion International has focused on holistic child development through sponsorship programs and microfinance loans designed to release children from economic, physical, social, and spiritual poverty. Compassion International is a Christ-centered, church-based, and child-focused organization partnering with over 7,500 churches across 25 countries.

https://www.compassion.com/

(To specify donations to go towards Compassion's Microfinance program, go to the "Additional Giving" option on the website. You will find "Other Donations," then you can pick "Income Generation" to give one time or monthly.)

ECLOF International

ECLOF began in 1946 with a vision to reconstruct churches in postwar Europe. Since then, it has expanded its reach to 13 countries in the developing world in  order to promote social justice and self-reliance through microfinance. ECLOF International is a network of socially driven microfinance institutions that provide financial and non-financial services to micro-entrepreneurs and smallholder farmers. ECLOF believes in a vision of a more equitable world, where all people are treated equally with a right to the dignity of leading fulfilled lives.

https://www.eclof.org/

Edify 501(c)(3)

Since 2009, Edify has helped more than 1 million students in eleven underserved countries around the world by coming alongside entrepreneurs who offer quality,  Christ-centered education to children living in underserved communities. Edify provides training to school leaders and teachers, access to capital for school owners, and access to education technology. Edify believes that educating underserved children is the greatest opportunity for Christian transformation in impoverished communities around the world.

https://www.edify.org/

Esperanza International 501(c)(3)

Since 1995, Esperanza has provided a comprehensive approach to poverty alleviation through access to capital, preventive healthcare and education, and financial and holistic services to restore hope and dignity in the Dominican Republic. Esperanza has disbursed over 250.000 loans, serving primarily women and Haitian immigrants. Esperanza was founded by MLB Player Dave Valle, with a heart for the underserved and a belief that all people, regardless of background, are God's children of equal worth.

https://esperanza.org/

HOPE International 501(c)(3)

Since 1997, HOPE International has invested in the dreams of underserved communities through discipleship, training, savings, and loans. HOPE serves over 1,000,000 clients in 16 countries around the world. HOPE's mission is to invest in the dreams of families in the world's underserved communities as they proclaim and live the gospel. In 2019, Charity Navigator awarded HOPE its highest rating (four stars) for the 12th consecutive year. (Less than 1 percent of organizations have accomplished this level of achievement.)

https://www.hopeinternational.org/

International Care Ministries (ICM) 501(c)(3)

For 25 years, ICM has combined the best practices of the business and academic worlds with the passion and heart of a faith-based nonprofit in order to help families living in ultrapoverty in the Philippines (those who live on less than 50 cents per person per day). ICM's vision is to release ultrapoor families from physical, emotional, and spiritual bondage through holistic training, medical treatments, meals, pastoral training, and savings groups through its Prevail program.

https://www.caremin.com/

Urwego Bank

Since 1997, Urwego Bank has shared the hope of Christ as it provides financial services and biblically based training designed to restore dignity and break the 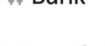 cycle of poverty in Rwanda. Urwego Bank's mission is to provide a ladder of opportunity to underserved communities in Rwanda as it proclaims and lives the gospel of Jesus Christ. Urwego Bank has distributed nearly $290 million in loans to underserved Rwandan entrepreneurs to promote sustainability, social transformation, and spiritual impact.

https://www.urwegobank.com/about-us/

VisionFund International 501(c)(3)

Since 2003, VisionFund has empowered families in 29 countries across Africa, Asia, Latin America, and the Middle East/Eastern Europe to create income  and jobs through financial services that enable clients to support their children and families. VisionFund believes in brighter futures for children and focuses on the poorest communities where loans can make the biggest impact. Working together with World Vision—a Christian relief, development, and advocacy organization—VisionFund enables communities to increase economic activity, to access clean water, education, and healthcare, to benefit from improvements to nutrition, and to provide the foundation for local economies to flourish.

http://www.visionfund.org

OTHER CHRIST-CENTERED ORGANIZATIONS

Beginning of Life

Beginning of Life was founded in 2000 with the initial goal of helping pregnant women save their babies. It's focus has grown since 2007 to include the fight against human trafficking and sexual violence in Moldova.

http://bol.md/

The Chalmers Center 501(c)(3)

The Chalmers Center was founded in 1999 by Dr. Brian Fikkert with a mission to equip local churches to break the bonds of poverty by moving away from

short-term handouts to lasting transformation. They believe poverty is not just a lack of material resources but a result of broken relationships. The Chalmers Center provides resources for local churches and ministries to love those living in poverty in biblical ways.

https://chalmers.org/

Invest Credit

Invest Credit is a Non-bank Credit Organization that responsibly and transparently provides loans in Moldova to better the lives of clients. Invest Credit also provides financial consultation to help clients achieve their dreams.

https://www.investcredit.md/

Open Gate International 501(c)(3)

Open Gate International is on a mission to combat human trafficking by offering training and mentoring for students to obtain

meaningful employment. Open Gate provides sustainable life skills training to empower students to develop a happy, healthy life and independent economic success.

https://opengateintl.org/

Salvation Army Moldova

For 25 years, The Salvation Army in Moldova has been serving the community through their youth and children programs, prison ministry, medical care for the elderly, and mobile clinic.

https://salvationarmy.md/

Tomorrow Clubs 501(c)(3)

Since 1997, Tomorrow Clubs has served small Eastern European communities devastated by decades of communism and desperate for the Good News of the gospel. Tomorrow Clubs provides a way for leaders from local churches

to engage lost kids in underserved communities through weekly club meetings. Tomorrow Clubs has shared the gospel with more than 250,000 children in eastern Europe.

https://tomorrowclubs.org/

Acknowledgments

This book has been a long time coming, mainly because it was a passion project rather than a professional endeavor. But also because it was a global effort! This project required countless hours of work from many individuals. It never would have come to life if not for an amazing team from all over the world, who walked alongside us to make it happen. We have deep, deep gratitude for the efforts of so many, and would like to express our huge thanks to a remarkable team that carried this project to completion since its inception more than three years ago.

Celina Kim, you were the glue that kept the whole thing moving forward. Part writer, part editor, part scheduler, part manager, part researcher … you wore so many hats, and always did so with ease and grace! Thank you for your servant's heart and graciousness in handling every request with a genuine willingness to help.

Steve Halliday, thank you for being our coach and guiding us from start to finish. Your expertise in this work was a huge comfort to lean on! Thank you for your contributions on so many levels—writing, editing, advising, resourcing—we're grateful to have had you as a steady guide, mentor, and coach along the way.

Rich Fox, thank you for the extraordinary work you did in helping us collect the data necessary to discover the conclusions we make in the book. It was remarkable to watch you uncover so many findings in the data, which were ultimately the basis of this book.

Josiah Kroontje, so glad you joined the team as we neared the finish line! You helped bring the whole thing home with your creative finesse.

Your efforts brought these stories to life in so many meaningful ways. Thank you for diving in and adding your unique touch to make this book what it is.

Bruce DeRoos, thank you for your artistic genius (as well as your patience with all of our back and forth) in making this book look stunning. From the cover to the page designs, your talents made this book look good!

Lindsey Hartz, we were so glad to have your marketing expertise as part of our team in order to help take this project to the next level. Thank you for jumping on board and pointing us in the right direction to make this book have the look and feel that will really resonate with readers. We also appreciate your help in getting it into the hands of readers.

And the lengths to which our friends around the globe went in order to help us meet the individuals whose stories are told in this book? Truly astounding. Andre Barkov, thank you for hosting me (Jenn) and Kevin and ensuring we had all the necessary meetings with your team and the clients you serve. Victor and Maksym, thank you for spending so much time with us and sharing your stories. Pasha, thank you for arranging visits to the saving groups so we could see what their lives are like and hear their stories. Luda, thank you for making it possible for us to understand- you helped us cross some major barriers!

Anastasia, you played a pivotal role in helping us obtain all of the content for the chapter on Moldova. It's because of you that we got connected to multiple people and organizations represented in this book. Thank you!

Anatol, thank you for being willing to meet us with very little context and for arranging all of the logistics for our Moldova visit. We gained a new friend and are so grateful for the connections you made which majorly influenced this book.

Serghei, Judy, Galina, Irina—thank you for meeting with us and for educating us on the global issue of human trafficking. And to the Moldovan factory workers and the lovely participants in the Moldovan culinary program—a huge thanks for letting us be a part of your world and understand your stories, lives, dreams, challenges, and hopes.

The HOPE International team—Jenna, Josiah, Dan, Rebecca, Erin, Brianna, Sarah Ann—thank you for all of your help in getting us necessary data and content for stories. Erin and Brianna, your help with editing was absolutely crucial to the formation of this book. Sarah Ann, thank you for seeking out and interviewing families whose stories are in the book.

Agaba and Jesse, thank you for using your personal time to help us collect powerful content representing Urwego and the amazing things that are happening in Rwanda. You went to great lengths to ensure we had all the necessary details—thank you!

And a huge thanks to those who helped us from day one as we refined our efforts and as the book took on a different form. Your encouragement as well as the initial stories you sent were instrumental in helping us determine what we wanted to accomplish with this book. Nicolas Karambadzakis, Ajay, Andre—thank you for the time and effort you spent collecting and sharing stories with us.

To our dear friends who were willing to read the book and give us honest and candid feedback—Pat, Chris, Peter, Addison, Mark—thank you! You helped shape the direction of the book as we neared final edits.

Belayneh, thank you for capturing Martha's story and for the days and hours you spent gathering the details that were both heart-wrenching and beautiful.

Hareg, we are so thankful for you sharing your story about Destiny Academy and continuing to fight for children.

The Compassion team—Marie and Pastor Johnny—we are so grateful for your efforts in helping us capture some inspiring stories from Haiti. Thank you for helping us coordinate across different countries and languages to get the inspiring stories told in this book.

The Center for Community Transformation (CCT) team—Lala, Silay, Rhodora, Malu—thank you for sticking with this project from the beginning and faithfully following up to help us get the information needed to represent you all in this book.

The Focus on the Family team—we so appreciate Jim Daly's support in writing the foreword, along with Doug Birnie, Kurt Leander, and Dan

Robbins assistance in orienting the material to speak into the lives of families and kids here in the US.

The VisionFund team—Darrel, Sara, Gary, Sophie—you all were also a part of this effort from the beginning. The data you provided was huge in helping us confirm our intuitions and see what the numbers have to say about the significance of Christ-centered microfinance. Thank you for the multiple phone calls (with a team all over the world), and for all of the back and forth as we sought to understand the data in meaningful ways.

The ICM team—Lincoln, Jansel, David—thank you for your help in getting hold of necessary data which you all have meticulously gathered over the years. It's remarkable what your team has been able to measure.

I (Jenn) would like to thank my husband, Kevin, for encouraging me every step of the way, and for supplying unrelenting support, no matter where in the world we went or what time I had to hop on a call or work on this project. To say "thank you" does not come close to conveying my deep gratitude for you serving as my faithful travel companion and accompanying me across the globe to conduct interviews. I love you!

Jeanie, you make me (Lance) better, and you're the best. Thanks for keeping me on track with our principles (e.g., Jesus always needs to be in the center), and for all of your time and patience. I love you and cherish you. Nate, Annalise, Christian, Bethie, & Abie—I know some of you are adopted, but I forget who. I love all of you. You're awesome!

Endnotes

Foreword

1. Investopedia, "Microfinance," from Investopedia website, https://www. investopedia.com/terms/m/microfinance.asp, accessed December 1, 2019.

1. Parent(s) + Opportunity = Kids Win

1. Brian Fikkert and Steve Corbett, When Helping Hurts: Alleviating Poverty Without Hurting the Poor … and Yourself (Chicago: Moody Publishers, 2009), 53.

2. Human Rights Watch, "US: Address Impact of Covid-19 on Poor," from Human Rights Watch website, https://www.hrw.org/ news/2020/03/19/us-address-impact-covid-19-poor, accessed March 20, 2020.

3. The World Bank, "The 2017 Global Findex: A Fresh Look at Reaching the Unbanked," from World Bank website, https://globalfindex. worldbank.org/sites/globalfindex/files/chapters/2017%20Findex%20 full%20report_chapter2.pdf, p. 35-41, accessed January 2, 2020.

4. Robert Cull and Jonathan Morduch, "Microfinance and Economic Development," World Bank Policy Research Working Paper No. 8252, November 2017, p. 1-35, available from NYU Wagner, accessed October 11, 2019.

5. HOPE International, "Annual Report 2018," from HOPE International website, https://www.hopeinternational.org/about-us/financials, p. 33, accessed October 11, 2019.

6. VisionFund International, "Annual Report 2018," from VisionFund website, https://www.visionfund.org/sites/default/files/2019-10/Vision Fund%20Annual%20Report%20FY18-Audit%20Report.pdf, p. 8, accessed October 11, 2019.

7. Howard Dayton, "Compass: 2,350 Verses on Money," Compass website, https://compass1.org/the-bible-on-money/, accessed March 9, 2020.

8. Matt. 6:21 (New International Version)

9. Wydick, Bruce. *Shrewd Samaritan: Faith, Economics, and the Road to Loving Our Global Neighbor*, (Nashville, Tennessee: W Publishing, 2019), 147-148.

10. Mrk. 10:14-15 (New International Version)

11. UNICEF and World Bank Group, Ending Extreme Poverty: A Focus on Children, Oct. 2016, p. 2, from UNICEF website, https://www.unicef.org/publications/files/Ending_Extreme_Poverty_A_Focus_on_Children_Oct_2016.pdf, accessed October 11, 2019.

12. VisionFund International, "Annual Report 2018," from VisionFund website, https://www.visionfund.org/sites/default/files/2019-10/VisionFund%20Annual%20Report%20FY18-Audit%20Report.pdf, p. 13, accessed October 11, 2019.

13. HOPE International, Annual Report 2018, from HOPE International website, https://www.hopeinternational.org/about-us/financials, accessed October 11, 2019.

14. The United Nations, "Household: Size & Composition, 2018," The United Nations website, https://population.un.org/Household/index.html#/countries/840, accessed October 11, 2019.

2. Kids Win Through Valuing Work

1. Lupton, Robert D. *Toxic Charity: How Churches and Charities Hurt Those They Help (and How to Reverse It)*, (New York, Harper One, 2001).

2. The World Bank, "The World Bank in Dominican Republic," The World Bank website, https://www.worldbank.org/en/country/dominicanrepublic/overview#1, accessed October 11, 2019.

3. BBC, "Dominican Republic profile-Overview," BBC website, https://www.bbc.com/news/world-latin-america-19246343, accessed October 11, 2019.

4. United Nations Development Programme "Human Development Indices and Indicators: 2018 Statistical Update Dominican Republic", p. 2, from UNDP website, http://hdr.undp.org/sites/all/themes/hdr_theme/country-notes/DOM.pdf, accessed October 11, 2019.

5. The United Nations, "Decent Work and Economic Growth: Why It Matters," the United Nations website, https://www.un.org/sustainabledevelopment/wp-content/uploads/2016/08/8.pdf, accessed February 1, 2020.

6. The United Nations, "Decent Work and Economic Growth: Why It Matters," the United Nations website, https://www.un.org/sustainabledevelopment/wp-content/uploads/2016/08/8.pdf, accessed February 1, 2020.

7. The United Nations, "Goal 8: Decent Work and Economic Growth," the United Nations website, https://www.undp.org/content/undp/en/home/sustainable-development-goals/goal-8-decent-work-and-economic-growth.html, accessed February 1, 2020.

8. The United Nations, "Decent Work and Economic Growth: Why It Matters," the United Nations website, https://www.un.org/sustainabledevelopment/wp-content/uploads/2016/08/8.pdf, accessed February 1, 2020.

9. Gordon B. Dahl, Adreas Ravndal Kostol, and Magne Mogstad, "Family Welfare Cultures," *The Quarterly Journal of Economics,* Vol. 129, Issue 4, November 2014, p. 1711-1752, accessed from Oxford Academic, accessed January 5, 2020.

3. Kids Win with Thriving Families: Can You Prevent a Broken Heart?

1. The World Bank, "The World Bank in Ethiopia," The World Bank website, https://www.worldbank.org/en/country/ethiopia/overview, October 11, 2019.

2. The World Bank, "The World Bank in Ethiopia," The World Bank website, https://www.worldbank.org/en/country/ethiopia/overview, October 11, 2019.

3. The World Bank, "The World Bank in Ethiopia," The World Bank website, https://www.worldbank.org/en/country/ethiopia/overview, October 11, 2019.

4. United Nations Development Programme, "Human Development Indices and Indicators: 2018 Statistical Update Ethiopia", p. 2, from UNDP website, http://hdr.undp.org/sites/all/themes/hdr_theme/country-notes/ETH.pdf, accessed October 11, 2019.

5. Emma Batha, "Factbox: Most children in orphanages are not orphans," Reuters website, https://www.reuters.com/article/us-slavery-conference-orphanages-factbox/factbox-most-children-in-orphanages-are-not-orphans-idUSKCN1NJ0AG, accessed March 12, 2020.

6. UNICEF and World Bank Group, Ending Extreme Poverty: A Focus on Children, Oct. 2016, p. 2, from UNICEF website, https://www.unicef.org/publications/files/Ending_Extreme_Poverty_A_Focus_on_Children_Oct_2016.pdf, accessed October 11, 2019.

7. UNICEF, "Orphans," from UNICEF website, https://www.unicef.org/media/media_45279.html, accessed March 10, 2020.

8. Emma Batha, "Factbox: Most children in orphanages are not orphans," Reuters, November 13, 2018, Reuters on the Web, https://www.reuters.com/article/us-slavery-conference-orphanages-factbox/factbox-most-children-in-orphanages-are-not-orphans-idUSKCN1NJ0AG, accessed March 12, 2020.

9. Alison Mutler, Gillian Wong, and David Crary, "Global effort to get kids out of orphanages gains momentum," AP News, December 19, 2017, AP on the Web, accessed March 12, 2020.

10. Alison Mutler, Gillian Wong, and David Crary, "Global effort to get kids out of orphanages gains momentum," AP News, December 19, 2017, AP on the Web, accessed March 12, 2020.

11. HOPE International, Annual Report 2018, from HOPE International website, https://www.hopeinternational.org/about-us/financials, p. 26, accessed October 11, 2019.

4. Kids Win with Sufficient Clothing: Using Scars to Heal

1. BBC, "Rwanda genocide: 100 days of slaughter," BBC website, https://www.bbc.com/news/world-africa-26875506, accessed October 11, 2019.

2. United Nations Development Programme "Human Development Indices and Indicators: 2018 Statistical Update Rwanda", p. 2, from UNDP website, http://hdr.undp.org/sites/all/themes/hdr_theme/country-notes/RWA.pdf, accessed October 11, 2019.

3.   BBC, "Rwanda genocide: 100 days of slaughter," BBC website, https://www.bbc.com/news/world-africa-26875506, accessed October 11, 2019.

4.   The World Bank, "Macro Poverty Outlook," October 2019, p. 270-271, from World Bank website, http://pubdocs.worldbank.org/en/366631492188168425/mpo-rwa.pdf, accessed October 11, 2019.

5.   United Nations Development Programme "Human Development Indices and Indicators: 2018 Statistical Update Rwanda", p. 2, from UNDP website, http://hdr.undp.org/sites/all/themes/hdr_theme/country-notes/RWA.pdf, accessed October 11, 2019.

6.   World Health Organization. "Soil-Transmitted Helminth Infections" 2013.

5. Kids Win with Spiritual Growth: A Beggar finds Jesus

1.   The World Health Organization, "Ukraine," The World Health Organization website, https://www.who.int/substance_abuse/publications/global_alcohol_report/profiles/ukr.pdf?ua=1, accessed January 2, 2020.

2.   Vanessa Gera and Mstyslav Chernov, "Ukrainian workers, seeing little hope at home, head abroad," *AP News,* March 25, 2019, AP News on the Web, accessed January 2, 2020.

3.   The United Nations, "Political solution 'long overdue' to protect the children of eastern Ukraine," The United Nations website, https://news.un.org/en/story/2019/12/105252, accessed January 2, 2020.

4.   The United Nations, "Political solution 'long overdue' to protect the children of eastern Ukraine," The United Nations website, https://news.un.org/en/story/2019/12/105252, accessed January 2, 2020.

5.   The World Bank, "Why Ukraine's Education System is Not Sustainable," The World Bank website, https://www.worldbank.org/en/news/opinion/2018/09/12/why-ukraines-education-system-is-not-sustainable, accessed January 2, 2020.

6.   The World Bank, "Why Ukraine's Education System is Not Sustainable," The World Bank website, https://www.worldbank.org/en/news/opinion/2018/09/12/why-ukraines-education-system-is-not-sustainable, accessed January 2, 2020.

7. Office for Democratic Institutions and Human Rights, "Situation Assessment Report: On Roma in Ukraine and the Impact of the Current Crisis," p.18, Office for Democratic Institutions and Human Rights, August 2014, available from OSCE website, accessed March 9, 2020.

8. Office for Democratic Institutions and Human Rights, "Situation Assessment Report: On Roma in Ukraine and the Impact of the Current Crisis," p.18, Office for Democratic Institutions and Human Rights, August 2014, available from OSCE website, accessed March 9, 2020.

9. Glenn Ellis and Viktoryia Kolchyna, "Attacked and abandoned: Ukraine's forgotten Roma," *Aljazeera,* November 23, 2018, Aljazeera on the Web, accessed March 9, 2020.

10. Glenn Ellis and Viktoryia Kolchyna, "Attacked and abandoned: Ukraine's forgotten Roma," *Aljazeera,* November 23, 2018, Aljazeera on the Web, accessed March 9, 2020.

11. Office for Democratic Institutions and Human Rights, "Situation Assessment Report: On Roma in Ukraine and the Impact of the Current Crisis," Office for Democratic Institutions and Human Rights, August 2014, available from OSCE website, accessed March 9, 2020.

12. Office for Democratic Institutions and Human Rights, "Situation Assessment Report: On Roma in Ukraine and the Impact of the Current Crisis," p.23-24 , Office for Democratic Institutions and Human Rights, August 2014, available from OSCE website, accessed March 9, 2020.

13. Henry Ridgwell, "Ukraine's Rural Villages Long for Government Help," VOA News, March 27, 2019, VOA News on the Web, accessed March 1, 2020.

14. The World Bank, "The World Bank In Ukraine," The World Bank website, https://www.worldbank.org/en/country/ukraine/overview#1, accessed October 11, 2019.

15. Reuters, "How Russia Took Crimea Without a Fight From Ukraine," *Newsweek,* July 24, 2017, *Newsweek* on the Web, accessed January 30, 2020.

16. History, "Ukraine declares its independence," History website, https://www.history.com/this-day-in-history/ukraine-declares-its-independence, accessed January 30, 2020.

17. Leonid Bershidsky, "Ukraine's Economy Enjoys a Hopeful Moment," *Bloomberg Green,* August 15, 2019, Bloomberg Green on the Web, accessed January 30, 2020.

18. United Nations Development Programme, "Human Development Reports Ukraine," United Nations Development Programme website, http://hdr. undp.org/en/countries/profiles/UKR, accessed October 11, 2019.

19. Central Intelligence Agency, "The World Factbook Ukraine," Central Intelligence Agency website, https://www.cia.gov/library/publications/ the-world-factbook/geos/up.html, accessed October 11, 2019.

20. George Barros, "The Russian Threat to Religious Freedom in Eastern Ukraine," *The Providence,* September 27, 2019, Providence Magazine on the Web, accessed October 11, 2019.

21. Corey Flintoff, "Ukrainian Protestants Say Religious Intolerance Rising in Donetsk," NPR, March 29, 2015, NPR on the Web, accessed March 20, 2020.

22. This methodology comes from The Chalmers Center, whose mission is to help churches and ministries discover better ways to love the poor, has created a curriculum, adopted by thousands of churches around the world, to help the poor take steps away from the entanglement of poverty and toward Jesus, community, and economic empowerment.

23. Pew Research Center, "One-in-Five U.S. Adults Were Raised in Interfaith Homes: A closer look at religious mixing in American families," Pew Research Center, October 26, 2016, available from Pew Research center website, accessed February 1, 2020.

24. Pew Research Center, "The Future of World Religions: Population Growth Projections, 2010-2050," April 2015, Pew Research Center website, https://www.pewforum.org/2015/04/02/religious-projections-2010-2050/, accessed October 11, 2019.

25. HOPE International, 2018 Annual Report, Dec. 2018, from HOPE International website, https://www.hopeinternational.org/documents/ financials/2018_AnnualReport_Digital_optimized.pdf

26. Rajeev Dehejia, Thomas DeLeire, Erzo F.P. Luttmer, and Joshua Mitchell, "The Role of Religious and Social Organizations in the Lives of Disadvantaged Youth," *The National Bureau of Economic Research Working Paper* No. 13369, September 2007, p. 29, available from National Bureau of Economic Research, accessed October 11, 2019.

6. Kids Win with Improved Housing: Francine the Ice Cream Lady

1. The World Bank, "The World Bank in Dominican Republic," The World Bank website, https://www.worldbank.org/en/country/dominicanrepublic/overview#1, accessed October 11, 2019.

2. BBC, "Dominican Republic profile-Overview," BBC website, https://www.bbc.com/news/world-latin-america-19246343, accessed October 11, 2019.

3. Yale University, "As Cities Grow, So Do The Numbers of the Homeless," Yale GlobalOnline website, https://yaleglobal.yale.edu/content/cities-grow-so-do-numbers-homeless, accessed October 11, 2019.

4. Habitat for Humanity, "7 Things You Should Know About Poverty and Housing," Habitat for Humanity website, https://www.habitat.org/stories/7-things-you-should-know-about-poverty-and-housing, accessed October 11, 2019.

5. Habitat for Humanity, "7 Things You Should Know About Poverty and Housing," Habitat for Humanity website, https://www.habitat.org/stories/7-things-you-should-know-about-poverty-and-housing, accessed October 11, 2019.

6. Habitat for Humanity, "7 Things You Should Know About Poverty and Housing," Habitat for Humanity website, https://www.habitat.org/stories/7-things-you-should-know-about-poverty-and-housing, accessed October 11, 2019.

7. Kids Win with Adequate Healthcare: I Just Put God First

1. The World Bank, "Malawi Data," the World Bank website, https://data.worldbank.org/country/malawi, accessed October 11, 2019.

2. United Nations Development Programme "Human Development Indices and Indicators: 2018 Statistical Update Malawi," from UNDP website, http://hdr.undp.org/sites/all/themes/hdr_theme/country-notes/MWI.pdf, accessed October 11, 2019.

3. Carlos Varela, Sven Young, Nyengo Mkandawire, Reinou S. Groen, Leonard Banza, Asgaut Viste, "Transportation Barriers to Access Health Care for Surgical Conditions in Malawi a cross sectional nationwide household survey," BMC Public Health 19, Article number 264, March 2019, available from BMC Public Health, accessed October 11, 2019.

4. The United Nations, "Good Health and Well-Being: Why It Matters," the United Nations website, https://www.un.org/sustainabledevelopment/wp-content/uploads/2017/03/ENGLISH_Why_it_Matters_Goal_3_Health.pdf, accessed October 11, 2019.

5. The United Nations, "Health," the United Nations website, https://www.un.org/en/sections/issues-depth/health/index.html, accessed October 11, 2019.

6. Office of Disease Prevention and Health Promotion, "Social Determinants of Health," Healthy People website, https://www.healthypeople.gov/2020/topics-objectives/topic/social-determinants-of-health, accessed March 20, 2020.

7. The United Nations, "Good Health and Well-being: Why It Matters," the United Nations website, https://www.un.org/sustainabledevelopment/wp-content/uploads/2017/03/ENGLISH_Why_it_Matters_Goal_3_Health.pdf, accessed October 11, 2019.

8. The United Nations, "Goal 3: Ensure healthy lives and promote well-being for all at all ages," the United Nations website, https://www.un.org/sustainabledevelopment/health/, accessed October 11, 2019.

9. The United Nations, "Good Health and Well-being: Why It Matters," the United Nations website, https://www.un.org/sustainabledevelopment/wp-content/uploads/2017/03/ENGLISH_Why_it_Matters_Goal_3_Health.pdf, accessed October 11, 2019.

8. Kids Win with Sufficient Food: Sink and Rise

1. United Nations Development Programme, "About the Philippines," UNDP website, http://www.ph.undp.org/content/philippines/en/home/countryinfo.html, accessed October 11, 2019.

2. United Nations Development Programme, "About the Philippines," UNDP website, http://www.ph.undp.org/content/philippines/en/home/countryinfo.html, accessed October 11, 2019.

3. The World Bank, "The World Bank in the Philippines," The World Bank website, https://www.worldbank.org/en/country/philippines/overview, accessed October 11, 2019.

4. United Nations Development Programme, "Human Development Indices and Indicators: 2018 Statistical Update Philippines," from UNDP website, http://hdr.undp.org/sites/all/themes/hdr_theme/country-notes/PHL.pdf, accessed October 11, 2019.

5. United Nations Development Programme, "About the Philippines," UNDP website, http://www.ph.undp.org/content/philippines/en/home/countryinfo.html, accessed October 11, 2019.

6. International Care Ministries, "2017-2018 Annual Report," International Care Ministries website, https://www.caremin.com/wp-content/uploads/2017/12/2017-2018_ICM_AR_WEB.pdf, accessed October 11, 2019.

7. The United Nations, "Sustainable Development Goals Goal 2: Zero Hunger," The United Nations website, https://www.un.org/sustainabledevelopment/hunger/, accessed October 11, 2019.

8. The United Nations, "Sustainable Development Goals Goal 2: Zero Hunger," The United Nations website, https://www.un.org/sustainabledevelopment/hunger/, accessed October 11, 2019.

9. The United Nations, "Sustainable Development Goals Goal 2: Zero Hunger," The United Nations website, https://www.un.org/sustainabledevelopment/hunger/, accessed October 11, 2019.

9. Kids Win with Basic Education: How Much Is a Dream Worth?

1. The World Bank, "Ethiopia Poverty Assessment," January 2015, The World Bank website, https://www.worldbank.org/en/topic/poverty/publication/ethiopia-poverty-assessment, accessed October 11, 2019.

2. The World Bank, "The World Bank In Ethiopia," The World Bank website, https://www.worldbank.org/en/country/ethiopia/overview, accessed October 11, 2019.

3. World Education News + Reviews, "Education in Ethiopia," World Education News + Reviews website, https://wenr.wes.org/2018/11/education-in-ethiopia, accessed October 11, 2019.

4. World Education News + Reviews, "Education in Ethiopia," World Education News + Reviews website, https://wenr.wes.org/2018/11/education-in-ethiopia, accessed October 11, 2019.

5. The United Nations, "Sustainable Development Goals Goal 4: Quality Education," The United Nations website, https://www.un.org/sustainabledevelopment/education/, accessed October 11, 2019.

6. The United Nations, "Sustainable Development Goals Goal 4: Quality Education," The United Nations website, https://www.un.org/sustainabledevelopment/education/, accessed October 11, 2019.

7. The United Nations, "Quality Education: Why It Matters," The United Nations website, https://www.un.org/sustainabledevelopment/wp-content/uploads/2017/02/4.pdf, accessed October 11, 2019.

8. The United Nations, "Quality Education: Why It Matters," The United Nations website, https://www.un.org/sustainabledevelopment/wp-content/uploads/2017/02/4.pdf, accessed October 11, 2019.

9. The United Nations, "Quality Education: Why It Matters," The United Nations website, https://www.un.org/sustainabledevelopment/wp-content/uploads/2017/02/4.pdf, accessed October 11, 2019.

10. Kids Win with Freedom from Trafficking: Better a Slave than Free?

1. Kelsey Hoie Ferrell, "History of Sex Trafficking in Moldova," End Slavery Now, February 9, 2016, *End Slavery Now* website, https://www.endslaverynow.org/blog/articles/history-of-sex-trafficking-in-moldova, accessed October 11, 2019.

2. International Organization for Migration, "World Migration Report 2018," 2017, available from IOM website, https://www.iom.int/wmr/world-migration-report-2018, accessed October 11, 2019.

3. United Nation and the Rule of Law, " Trafficking in Persons," United Nations website, https://www.un.org/ruleoflaw/thematic-areas/transnational-threats/trafficking-in-persons/, accessed October 11, 2019.

4. United Nations Office on Drugs and Crime, "Human Trafficking," United Nations Office on Drugs and Crimes website, https://www.unodc.org/unodc/en/human-trafficking/what-is-human-trafficking.html, accessed October 11, 2019.

5. The World Bank, "The World Bank In Moldova," The World Bank website, https://www.worldbank.org/en/country/moldova/overview, accessed October 11, 2019.

6. International Labour Office, "Migrant Workers: The Case of Moldova," 2017, p. 7, available from ILO website, https://www.ilo.org/wcmsp5/ groups/public/---ed_protect/---protrav/---migrant/documents/ publication/wcms_613508.pdf, accessed October, 11, 2019.

7. Minnesota Advocates for Human Rights, Trafficking in Women: Moldova and Ukraine, December 2000, p. 39, Minnesota Advocates for Human Rights website, https://www.theadvocatesforhumanrights.org/uploads/ traffickingreport_2.pdf, accessed October 11, 2019.

8. Kaunain Rahman, "Moldova: Overview of corruption and anti-corruption with a focus on the healthcare and procurement sectors," U4, September 27, 2017, available from U4, accessed October 11, 2019.

9. Alexander Clapp, "Moldova's Drama on the Dniester," The National Interest, December 18, 2015, The National Interest on the Web, accessed October 11, 2019.

10. Maria Dulgher, "Why the citizens of the Republic of Moldova are not protected by the rule of law or the moment when the equal justice crushed," Moldova.org, March 27, 2019, available from Moldolva.org on the Web, accessed January 2, 2020.

11. The Inter-Agency Coordination Group against Trafficking in Persons, Issue Brief #4 The Gender Dimensions of Human Trafficking, September 2017, from The Inter-Agency Coordination Group against Trafficking in Persons website, http://icat.network/sites/default/files/publications/ documents/ICAT-IB-04-V.1.pdf ,accessed January 2, 2020.

12. Institute for Women's Policy Research, "The Economic Drivers and Consequences of Sex Trafficking in the United States," September 2017, p. 2, available from IWPR website, https://iwpr.org/wp-content/ uploads/2017/09/B369_Economic-Impacts-of-Sex-Trafficking-BP-3.pdf, accessed January 30, 2020.

13. United Nations Office on Drugs and Crime, Global Report on Trafficking in Persons 2014, November 2014, p. 1, from United Nations Office on Drugs and Crime website, https://www.unodc.org/documents/data-and-analysis/glotip/GLOTIP_2014_full_report.pdf, accessed October 11, 2019.

14. Human Rights First, "Human Trafficking by the Numbers," Human Rights First website, https://www.humanrightsfirst.org/resource/human-trafficking-numbers, accessed January 30, 2020.

15. United Nations Office on Drugs and Crime, Global Report on Trafficking in Persons 2014, November 2014, p. 1, from United Nations Office on Drugs and Crime website, https://www.unodc.org/documents/data-and-analysis/glotip/GLOTIP_2014_full_report.pdf, accessed October 11, 2019.

16. United Nations Office on Drugs and Crime, Global Report on Trafficking in Persons 2014, November 2014, p. 1, from United Nations Office on Drugs and Crime website, https://www.unodc.org/documents/data-and-analysis/glotip/GLOTIP_2014_full_report.pdf, accessed October 11, 2019.

17. United Nations Office on Drugs and Crime, Global Report on Trafficking in Persons 2014, November 2014, p. 1, from United Nations Office on Drugs and Crime website, https://www.unodc.org/documents/data-and-analysis/glotip/GLOTIP_2014_full_report.pdf, accessed October 11, 2019.

11. Kids Win with Post-Disaster Rebuilding: A Crucial Stepping Stone

1. World Vision, "2010 Haiti earthquake: Facts, FAQs, and how to help," World Vision website, https://www.worldvision.org/disaster-relief-news-stories/2010-haiti-earthquake-facts#challenges-today, accessed October 11, 2019.

2. Corey Flintoff, "In Post-Quake Haiti, A Surge of Amputees," NPR, February 12, 2010, NPR website, accessed October 11, 2019.

3. The World Bank, "The World Bank In Haiti," The World Bank website, https://www.worldbank.org/en/country/haiti/overview, accessed October 11, 2019.

4. The World Bank, "Poverty & Equity Brief: Haiti," The World Bank website, https://databank.worldbank.org/data/download/poverty/33EF03BB-9722-4AE2-ABC7-AA2972D68AFE/Global_POVEQ_HTI.pdf, accessed April 13, 2020.

5. The World Bank, "The World Bank In Haiti," The World Bank website, https://www.worldbank.org/en/country/haiti/overview, accessed October 11, 2019.

6. World Vision, "2010 Haiti earthquake: Facts, FAQs, and how to help," World Vision website, https://www.worldvision.org/disaster-relief-news-stories/2010-haiti-earthquake-facts#challenges-today, accessed October 11, 2019.

7. Owen Bennett-Jones, "Has the international community failed Haiti?," BBC, August 7, 2015, *BBC* website, accessed October 11, 2019.

8. Owen Bennett-Jones, "Has the international community failed Haiti?," BBC, August 7, 2015, *BBC* website, accessed October 11, 2019.

9. Owen Bennett-Jones, "Has the international community failed Haiti?," BBC, August 7, 2015, *BBC* website, accessed October 11, 2019.

10. Compassion International, "About Us," Compassion International website, https://www.compassion.com/about/about-us.htm, accessed October 11, 2019.

11. World Health Organization, "Natural event," June 14, 2019, World Health Organization website,https://www.who.int/environmental_health_emergencies/natural_events/en/, accessed October 11, 2019.

12. Charlotte Benson and Edward Clay, "Economic and Financial Impacts of Natural Disasters: an Assessment of Their Effects and Options for Mitigation: Synthesis Report", May 2003, available from Overseas Development Institute website, https://www.odi.org/sites/odi.org.uk/files/odi-assets/publications-opinion-files/6149.pdf, accessed February 1, 2020.

12. Kids Win: Calculating the Impact

1. The United States Census Bureau, "U.S. and World Population Clock," the United States Census Bureau website, https://www.census.gov/popclock/, accessed on February 2, 2020.

2. The World Bank, "Financial Inclusion on the Rise, But Gaps Remain, Global Findex Database Shows," the World Bank website, https://www.worldbank.org/en/news/press-release/2018/04/19/financial-inclusion-on-the-rise-but-gaps-remain-global-findex-database-shows, accessed on February 1, 2020.

3. The World Bank, "Poverty," the World Bank website, https://www.worldbank.org/en/topic/poverty/overview, accessed on February 1, 2020.

4. The World Bank, "Poverty and Shared Prosperity 2018: Piecing Together the Poverty Puzzle," the World Bank website, https://www.worldbank.org/en/publication/poverty-and-shared-prosperity, accessed on February 1, 2020.

5. Roy Katayama and Divyanshi Wadhwa, "Half of the world's poor live in just 5 countries," the World Bank Blog website, http://blogs.worldbank.org/opendata/half-world-s-poor-live-just-5-countries, accessed on February 1, 2020.

6. The United Nations, "Report of the Special Rapporteur on extreme poverty and human rights on his mission to the United States of American," United Nations General Assembly, May 2018, available from the United Nations website, accessed February 1, 2020.

7. Giving USA, "Giving USA 2018: American Gave $410.02 Billion to Charity in 2017, Crossing the $400 Billion Mark for the First Time," Giving USA, June 14, 2019, Giving USA website, https://givingusa.org/giving-usa-2018-americans-gave-410-02-billion-to-charity-in-2017-crossing-the-400-billion-mark-for-the-first-time/, accessed February 1, 2020.

8. Charity Navigator, "Giving Statistics," Charity Navigator website, https://www.charitynavigator.org/index.cfm?bay=content.view&cpid=42, accessed February 1, 2020.

9. Conrad Hackett and David McClendon, "Christians remain world's largest religious group, but they are declining in Europe," *Pew Research Center,* April 5, 2017, Pew Research Center on the Web, accessed February 2, 2020.

10. HOPE International, "Annual Report 2018," from HOPE International website, https://www.hopeinternational.org/about-us/financials, p. 5, accessed October 11, 2019.

11. International Care Ministries, "2018-2019 Annual Report," International Care Ministries website, https://www.caremin.com/wp-content/uploads/2018/12/2018ICM-AR-FINAL_Web.pdf, p. 12, accessed February 2, 2020.

12. International Care Ministries, "2018-2019 Annual Report," International Care Ministries website, https://www.caremin.com/wp-content/uploads/2018/12/2018ICM-AR-FINAL_Web.pdf, p. 12, accessed February 2, 2020.

13. International Care Ministries, "2018-2019 Annual Report," International Care Ministries website, https://www.caremin.com/wp-content/uploads/2018/12/2018ICM-AR-FINAL_Web.pdf, p. 2, accessed February 2, 2020.

14. VisionFund, Vision Fund Annual Report 2018, from VisionFund website, https://www.wvi.org/publications/economic-development/visionfund-annual-report-2018, p. 10, accessed February 1, 2020.

15. VisionFund, Vision Fund Annual Report 2018, from VisionFund website, https://www.wvi.org/publications/economic-development/visionfund-annual-report-2018, p . 10, accessed February 1, 2020.

16. VisionFund, Vision Fund Annual Report 2018, from VisionFund website, https://www.wvi.org/publications/economic-development/visionfund-annual-report-2018, p. 3, accessed February 1, 2020.

17. HOPE International, Annual Report 2018, from HOPE International website, https://www.hopeinternational.org/about-us/financials, accessed October 11, 2019.

18. HOPE International, Annual Report 2018, from HOPE International website, https://www.hopeinternational.org/about-us/financials, p. 31, accessed October 11, 2019.

19. HOPE International, Annual Report 2018, from HOPE International website, https://www.hopeinternational.org/about-us/financials, p. 8-9, accessed October 11, 2019.

20. The United Nations, "Household Size & Composition, 2019," United Nations website, https://population.un.org/Household/index.html#/countries/646, accessed February 1, 2020.

21. VisionFund International, *CWBO Highlight_FY17*, V2 (2018), distributed by VisionFund International.

22. VisionFund International, *CWBO Highlight_FY17*, V2 (2018), distributed by VisionFund International.

23. VisionFund International, *CWBO Highlight_FY17*, V2 (2018), distributed by VisionFund International.

24. VisionFund International, *CWBO Highlight_FY17*, V2 (2018), distributed by VisionFund International.

25. VisionFund International, *CWBO Full FY 18 Myanmar Data,* (2018), distributed by VisionFund International.

26. VisionFund International, *CWBO Full FY 18 Myanmar Data*, (2018), distributed by VisionFund International.

27. VisionFund International, *CWBO Full FY 18 Myanmar Data*, (2018), distributed by VisionFund International.

28. VisionFund International, *CWBO Full FY 18 Myanmar Data*, (2018), distributed by VisionFund International.

29. VisionFund International, *CWBO Highlight_FY17*, V2 (2018), distributed by VisionFund International.

30. Collins, Jim. *Good to Great: Why Some Companies Make the Leap... and Others Don't,* (New York, NY: HarperCollins Publishers Inc., 2001).

31. Expert Program Management, "Book Summary: Good to Great by Jim Collins," EPM website, https://expertprogrammanagement.com/2018/05/good-to-great-collins-summary/, accessed February 2, 2020.

32. Wydick, Bruce. *Shrewd Samaritan: Faith, Economics, and the Road to Loving Our Global Neighbor* (Nashville, Tennessee: W Publishing, 2019).

33. Wydick, Bruce. *Shrewd Samaritan: Faith, Economics, and the Road to Loving Our Global Neighbor,* (Nashville, Tennessee: W Publishing, 2019), 104.

34. Wydick, Bruce. *Shrewd Samaritan: Faith, Economics, and the Road to Loving Our Global Neighbor,* (Nashville, Tennessee: W Publishing, 2019), 105.

35. VisionFund, "VisionFund Cambodia sold to Woori Bank of Korea," VisionFunds website, https://www.visionfund.org/newsroom/visionfund-cambodia-sold-woori-bank-korea, accessed February 2, 2020.

36. Wydick, Bruce. *Shrewd Samaritan: Faith, Economics, and the Road to Loving Our Global Neighbor,* (Nashville, Tennessee: W Publishing, 2019), 148.

13. How You Win, Too

1. Eph. 2:10 (New International Version)

2. Thess. 5:16-18 (New International Version)

3. Psa. 107:1 (New International Version)

4. The World Bank, "Financial Inclusion on the Rise, But Gaps Remain, Global Findex Database Shows," The World Bank website, https://www.worldbank.org/en/news/press-release/2018/04/19/financial-inclusion-on-the-rise-but-gaps-remain-global-findex-database-shows, accessed February 1, 2020.

5. The World Bank, "Poverty," The World Bank website, https://www.worldbank.org/en/topic/poverty/overview, accessed February 1, 2020.

6. Gary Rivlin, "In Silicon Valley, Millionaires Who Don't Feel Rich," *The New York Times,* August 5, 2007, The New York Times on the Web, accessed February 19, 2020.

7. Global Rich List, "Income," Global Rich List website, http://www.globalrichlist.com/, accessed January 1, 2020.

8. Soyoung Q. Park, Thorsten Kahnt, Azade Dogan, Sabrina Strang, Ernst Fehr, and Philippe N. Tobler, "A neural link between generosity and happiness," *Nature Communications,* July 2017, p. 1-10, available from Nature, accessed February 20, 2020.

9. 2 Cor. 9:6 (New International Version)

10. Soyoung Q. Park, Thorsten Kahnt, Azade Dogan, Sabrina Strang, Ernst Fehr, and Philippe N. Tobler, "A neural link between generosity and happiness," *Nature Communications,* July 2017, p. 6, available from Nature, accessed February 20, 2020.

11. Mrk. 12:41-44 (New International Version)

12. Eph. 2:8-9 (New International Version)

13. Jhn. 5:11-12 (New International Version)

14. 1 Cor. 3:11-14 (New International Version)

15. Matt. 6:9-20 (New International Version)